Prayer and Personal Religion

✝

Prayer
—— *and* ——
Personal Religion

John B. Coburn

revised and updated by Richard H. Schmidt

 Morehouse Publishing
Harrisburg – New York

 FORWARD
MOVEMENT
Cincinnati

Unless otherwise noted, the scripture quotations contained herein are from
the New Revised Standard Version Bible, copyright © 1989 by the Division
of Christian Education of the National Council of Churches of Christ in the
U.S.A. Used by permission. All rights reserved.

Library of Congress Cataloging-in-Publication Data
Coburn, John B.
Prayer and personal religion / by John B. Coburn ; revised and updated by
Richard H. Schmidt.
       p.   cm.
ISBN 978-0-8192-2358-6 (pbk.)
1. Prayer—Christianity. I. Schmidt, Richard H., 1944– II. Title.
BV210.3.C62 2009
248.3'2—dc22

                                          2008052105

Cover design by Jennifer Glosser
Interior design by Vicki K. Black

Printed in the United States of America.

Morehouse Publishing   Forward Movement
4775 Linglestown Road   300 W. Fourth Street
Harrisburg, PA 17112   Cincinnati, OH 45202

Morehouse Publishing
445 Fifth Avenue
New York, NY 10016

Morehouse Publishing is an imprint of Church Publishing Incorporated.

09 10 11 12 13 14   10 9 8 7 6 5 4 3 2

Table of Contents

✝

Foreword

It comes to me as a joyful surprise that this little book on prayer is being reissued a half century after it was written. Although much has changed in the world, in our culture, and in the church since its first publication, this re-publication suggests that there is something timeless about our longing for a meaningful relationship with God, and that the essential task of prayer remains simple and constant from generation to generation. God's reaching out to us and our response is the most basic dynamic of being human.

I suggest in this book that it is God himself who teaches us to pray, who leads us down the particular path of our life and shapes our inner self. After fifty years I continue to believe deeply that this is true. Prayer is not so much a matter of forms and practices, although forms and practices can be important, as it is a matter of consistent openness to the creative spirit of God in our hearts, a spirit which is infinitely alive across the stages and specific adventures and circumstances of our lives.

I am very grateful to all of the companions I have had in my life who have supported and nurtured my own life in prayer. I am grateful, too, to Forward Movement and Church Publishing Incorporated for making this new edition possible. I hope that this little book can continue to be of service to individuals in the development of their own lives of prayer.

JOHN B. COBURN
Bedford, Massachusetts
June 2008

Preface

It was nearly forty years ago that I first picked up John Coburn's *Prayer and Personal Religion*. A newly ordained priest, I was fresh out of the seminary where I had studied academic ideas about God. But the parishioners of my little parish in eastern West Virginia were not interested in ideas *about* God: they wanted to know God personally, and I felt ill-equipped to make the introduction. The problem was that I had not learned to pray. When I came across this book, I hoped it would teach me what my parishioners wanted me to teach them.

The book was what I needed. As I have grown and as times have changed, the method and content of my praying has changed as well, but it was John Coburn's little book that got me started. Its practical, down-to-earth, honest approach made the life of prayer feel, for the first time, possible for me. Prayer no longer seemed ethereal, daunting, heavy, or boring, but something I felt I might actually enjoy. And so I have, for most of the past forty years.

In editing *Prayer and Personal Religion* for this new edition, I have sought to update Coburn's text for the twenty-first century, while retaining as much as possible of the original. The ideas and virtually all the wording are Coburn's. In keeping with current literary norms, I have condensed some sentences and broken some long sentences into shorter ones. The only substantial change has been an updating of the bibliography in chapter 6.

It has been a pleasure and an honor to revisit this excellent text and to prepare it for republication. I hope it may prove as useful for prayerful Christians of the next generation as it has been for me in my generation.

RICHARD H. SCHMIDT
Cincinnati, Ohio
June 2008

✝

CHAPTER 1

Prayer Is Response to God

The purpose of this volume is to help you pray and grow in your personal religious life. It is a book about your inner life and your relationship with God. Although this relationship is unique for each person, there is a general way in which God deals with us and through which we respond. This book is concerned with this general pattern. I hope that as you read it you will come to understand how God is already dealing with you personally and therefore respond more fully to him. This is how most of us come finally to discover that it is God himself who teaches us best to pray.

Prayer is response to God. The first step is God's. He begins the relationship with us, and when we pray, we make our response. If you have ever prayed, you have already responded to God. Indeed, if you have even *wanted* to pray, you have responded. In either case it is a sign that God has already touched you. And if you have never prayed, it may be because you have not recognized God's touch.

Look for a moment at some of the ways God touches people. You may recognize some of these experiences as your own. God may already have done more in your life than you suspect.

Have you, for example, ever stood outdoors at night looking up into the heavens? It is a brilliantly clear night and the stars stand out so distinctly that you feel you could almost reach up and touch one. Gazing at this canopy, you are overwhelmed by the immensity and greatness and mysterious order of the universe, and with your own tiny insignificance in contrast. If you have had this experience, both exalting you and humbling you at the same time, God may have touched you, for this is one of the ways God breaks in on people.

A similar experience is described by a young college graduate: "In recent years," he writes, "I have been struck by my inability to direct my life according to my own best intentions. I find myself caught in patterns of behavior I had firmly resolved to avoid. I discover a weakness within myself which I had not been aware of. At the same time, when I go on long walks in the country, which has always been a pleasure of mine, I have a vague, uneasy sense that something else or someone else is trying to communicate with me. So I ask, 'What goes on here?'" If you have ever felt confronted by some such sense of "otherness," which is frequently mysterious and awesome and perhaps even frightening, you have experienced one of the ways God breaks through to a person's consciousness.

Some people recognize God first simply through a sense of duty. One man, explaining how he coped with the loss of his wife and two of his children, said, "At that time I discovered life was spelling out for me a four-letter word, d-u-t-y. So I have tried ever since to do my duty to my colleagues, my family, and my community." Eventually he came to relate these duties to God. So wherever there is an "ought" in your life, when you have nothing to go on except what you know is "right," God is touching you.

Again, if you have ever suspected that the only problem you really have is yourself—not somebody or something else—that may be God trying to get your attention. It is called guilt. You may not know just what you're guilty of or who is judging you, but you have a persistent gnawing, uneasy feeling. God may be responsible for that feeling; it is an opening though which you can turn to him.

Or take a different kind of experience. You may have been taken quite out of yourself and been "transported into another world." This happens in all parts of the world, to both religious and secular-minded people. It can happen when someone is confronted by sheer beauty—a sunset or a work of art or a beautiful woman—or when someone is "carried away" by great music or "lost" in contemplating a magnificent idea. Men and women are "inspired" to become more than they normally are when brought face to face with saints, or when they fall in love. There is often a sense of yearning or longing for something the world cannot give. These experiences come from God. If you have had such an "inspiration," you have been touched by him.

Some people are also drawn to God through religion, the persistent appeal of the Bible and the church. Even those who have turned away from organized religion sometimes feel an inner restlessness that causes them to look wistfully at the Christian faith and things that represent God. They may read the Bible off and on for years or occasionally attend a worship service. You may have known this peculiar fascination with either the Bible or the church. It is one of the ways God touches people.

Who Is God?

These, then, are some of the human experiences through which God breaks into people's lives. If you have ever experienced these things and have prayed, or even wanted to pray, you have been touched by God and responded to him. You may not have known it then. You may have difficulty believing it now. But this is the starting place: prayer is response to God. Prayer is always the second step, our response to the initiative taken by God.

Who is this God to whom we respond? How do you picture God—as a policeman, or a judge, or a kindly old grandfather, or a remote First Cause? These are common ideas of God—and they are all wrong. Such false ideas of God cause havoc in people's lives. If you begin with a wrong idea of God, then you get the wrong idea of yourself and of other people and of the relation of God to them—and you are in trouble.

Here is another picture of God. It is not entirely accurate, of course, because human words can never describe

God perfectly. It is a rough picture, a simple one, only approximately true, but it fits with Christian understandings. Think of God in some such way as this. It may take some believing at the outset, but remember that you can never get into trouble by thinking thoughts of God that are too great.

God is a Person. He is infinitely more than this, but he is at least this. That is where to begin, for if you think of God as a Person, when you speak to him you can say "you" and "I." When God addresses you, he in turn speaks to a person and also says "you." Thus a two-way personal conversation is begun, set in a personal relationship. This personal conversation is the essence of prayer.

God is a Person who thinks and acts. His thoughts and actions are perfect. He always "does the truth" and his works are without fail beautiful and good. God is responsible for joy and peace in our hearts. His actions in and through people and nature always have such characteristics as these.

Best of all, however, God is a *loving* Person. Love is the reason God founded the world and created everything in it. He loves everybody everywhere all the time. God created *you* because he loves you. Think of God as loving you as though you are the only person in the world. That is how much God loves you, and what he wants above all else is for you to love him in return. You know from your experience of human love that that is what a lover always wants: for the beloved to respond with love.

God has been trying, in all the experiences of your life, so to touch you that you will turn to him and love him. He has been striving to break through not only in the out-of-the-ordinary experiences mentioned above, but in all the events and relationships of your life—of love and peace, sorrow and death, guilt and sin, beauty and joy. *Everything you have ever experienced has been God trying to communicate with you.* God is doing everything possible to bridge what separates you from him. As we shall see, God will stop at nothing that is not contrary to his nature—not even the death of his Son—so that you and he may come together and converse with each other, saying "I" and "you," that you may know God as your lover and yourself as his beloved.

If you can get this kind of picture of God, you have enough to begin. There are experiences in your life that can best be understood as God trying to touch you. They begin to make sense because now, perhaps for the first time, you see God in them. Through them he has found you. Indeed, you would not have read this page if God had not already found you.

You may conclude this chapter with an experiment to see for yourself what God has already done in your life. The experiment has two steps:

> 1. Take this present moment and ask yourself: What are the good things in my life for which I am not responsible? Make a list: your life itself, someone who loves you and trusts you, your intelligence, your parents and family background, work to do, friends—what else? Make your list. Now say:

Everything good in my life that I am not responsible for, God is responsible for.

2. Now write down all the things in your life you consider evil. What are they? Sickness, failures, death of loved ones, misunderstandings, hopes broken, your sins (do not slide over these; be specific)—what else? Make your list. Now say: *Everything in my life that I consider evil, God permits.*

What are your findings? Can you point to any good in your life that God is responsible for? Can you see any evil that God permits for a special purpose? If you answer *yes* to either question, that is where God is touching you now. From this place you can turn to him in response to his initiative. This is the beginning of a personal relationship which is started by God and continues as you come to know and love and serve him.

Your prayer is your response. It is the second step. The first step was God's and has already been taken.

The way to begin is to say at this moment, "O God, *you.* . . ." Once you have said "God, *you,*" and not "God, *he,*" you have begun to pray. This is your response to God. Prayer is always response to God. You can take this second step now.

"O God, I have this to say to *you.* . . . What have you to say to *me?*"

CHAPTER 2

Be Yourself and Begin Where You Are

It seems strange, but God does not mind being our last choice. We dislike even being second choice, like in a pick-up ballgame or on a guest list for dinner. But God is content to be last choice.

This chapter is for people who make God their last choice. If you have tried other ways of living, apart from God, and found them wanting, this chapter is for you. Suppose you have made the experiment at the end of the previous chapter and now decide to respond to God. There are two simple rules to follow at the beginning. The first one is: *Be yourself.*

Be natural before God. Do not pretend to be what you are not or to feel emotions you do not feel. Tell God what is really on your heart, with whatever words are most natural to you. You don't have to use "religious" language or speak of "spiritual" matters only. We shall see how the great prayers of the ages, clothed in majestic language, can help us, but when you begin, speak naturally and easily, as you would to a friend, since God is just that. Be yourself.

Being yourself goes deeper than language. It probes the depths of your feelings about God and the circumstances of your life. You don't have to feel "pious" or "holy" or "spiritual." Just be honest. Let God hear what you are really feeling. If you are resentful because someone you love has died, do not say with your lips, "O God, thy will be done," when in your heart you are saying, "You have done a terrible thing and what an awful God you are!" Dishonesty sets up smoldering resentment and will break out destructively sooner or later.

The important thing is to tell God exactly how you do feel: "O God, I hate you for this! You are so unjust, so heartless! If this is what you are really like, I'm through with you before we begin!" The Book of Psalms is the Bible's prayer book, and many of the psalms ooze with anger, bitterness, confusion, despair, doubt, and mean-spiritedness. God has heard it all before and he can take it.

You cannot cover up before God. Express yourself just as you are—not as you imagine God (or somebody else) says you ought to be. *Honesty at the outset is required if you are to go on to a creative, free, and mature relationship with God.*

A young father sat grim-faced through the funeral of his four-year-old son. As he listened to the opening words, "I know that my Redeemer lives," he kept murmuring under his breath: "God, I'll get back at you for this! I'll get back at you for this!"

This was the first honest conversation he had ever had with God. Later he commented: "That was a foolish thing to say, I suppose. How could I ever get back at God? Yet it was honest and it kept the relationship with God open. That was how I felt and it cleared the air to get it off my chest. When I gradually came to myself, I saw that death has to go into some final framework and only God can absorb it. I read and reread all those experiences of people suffering before God, especially Job, and in time his sentiments became mine, or almost mine. I know now that my Redeemer *does* live. And I don't think I would know it, deep down inside, if I hadn't been mad at my Redeemer once—and said so."

So be yourself; do not pretend. That is the only way to respond to God. Anyhow, to try to hide anything from God is a waste of time. He already knows what is in your heart. God knows who you truly are, so *be* who you truly are. In the words of an ancient prayer, God is the one "unto whom all hearts are open, all desires known, and from whom no secrets are hid." That means *your* heart, *your* desires, *your* secrets.

The second rule is this: *Begin where you are.* Look at what you need to have a completely fulfilled life. Most people begin to pray because they need:

- peace of mind

- power for living

- to be forgiven.

Let's take a brief look at each of these. You may want *peace of mind* so that you can accept life. You need to learn to take all that life does to you. You search for an inner composure and calm, for a basic stability when the storms blow and sickness, sufferings, sorrow, defeats, and failures descend. You long for a peace that overcomes your fears and anxieties.

This search for peace of mind seldom arises from material needs or wants. Often the outwardly prosperous are the most fearful. A young insurance man, the most successful agent in a large company, in a burst of confidence, said, "I am a fear-ridden man. I am afraid I shall be an utter failure. I fear I shall get no prospects; when I do, I'm afraid I shall lose them. Once they are signed, I'm afraid they won't pass their physical examinations or pay their premiums. No big fears—I'm just riddled with little fears." He concluded: "If anybody ever needed religion, believe me, I'm the fellow. Nobody else seems able to help me; maybe God can."

You may be one of those who turn to God out of your need for peace of mind. If so, begin by telling God of your need and ask frankly and deliberately for help.

Or you may be looking for *power for living.* Your life has gone along so far and then you have run out of gas. The tasks of living seem too great for you, the demands too much. The ball comes over the plate too fast. Some will say, "I can't seem to get my feet off the ground," and others, "I always seem to be up in the air." They both mean the same thing: the sense of purposefulness in life is gone; there is no power.

This is a problem of middle age more than any other. The physical satisfactions have begun to dwindle. You realize that you will not solve all the problems of human existence. Your enthusiasm wanes. You have long since compromised earlier ideals and abandoned youthful hopes. You begin to settle down to mediocrity and life "as it really is."

Boredom sets in, coupled with restlessness. You find yourself on a treadmill and realize you have been there for a long time—too much rushing for commuter trains, too many harried business conferences, too many lost golf balls, too many martinis, too much television (*anything* to relieve the boredom), too many divorces. The kicks are gone.

It is a sound instinct that declares: "There must be more to life than this!" Beneath these surface phenomena is a deep urge to make your life count, to direct it to some creative purpose, to clothe it with dignity and meaning. If there is no place else to go, no one else to turn to, you turn to God for the power to live. If this is you, turn and ask God for help.

If it is neither peace of mind nor power for living that you need, you probably know that you need, above all else, *to be forgiven.* There is no neat three-way division here, for we all belong in varying degrees in all three groups. The most basic need, however, intimately bound up with the other two, is to be made clean.

Looking back over the years, you see what has gradually happened. Perhaps it began with the exciting challenge of seeing how much you could get away with. Then came the foolish, reckless acts of youth and the indulgences of the flesh. More dangerous was the casual compromise with truth and the occasional deliberate lie to protect yourself. And all along there were outbursts of temper and petty acts of selfishness. Worst of all, you hurt the people you loved most and turned your back on opportunities to show them your love. And now, most of the time, you think mainly about yourself, your wants, your reputation.

You can fill in the details. They add up to a great burden of guilt. It is this weight, more than any other, that slows you down and robs you of your peace of mind and power for living. This is the burden from which you long to be freed. No psychiatrist or human agent can lift it from you—but God can and will. He will forgive you and make you clean—if you turn to him and ask him.

When we confront our need for forgiveness, we are close to the very heart of Christian faith. Stated bluntly, we are all in trouble because we are all separated from God. That is what sin is. Once we confess it, God takes it away and we are right with him. And once made clean, we receive the keys to peace of mind and power for living.

These, then, are our needs—peace of mind, power for living, to be forgiven. When you know what you need, you are ready to pray. Don't worry about its being a "selfish" need. It may be. But if you know it, God knows it. Your beginning prayers can be "selfish" prayers. They are the initial lines of communication with God, and as such are of crucial importance. They will change their character as your prayer continues and time goes on. There is nothing wrong with such prayers any more than there is something wrong with a toddler's halting first steps. You begin where you are; you could hardly begin anywhere else. Then you move on with firmer steps as you grow to maturity.

THE FIRST THREE PRAYERS

So begin. God is your choice. You have responded and begun to pray. Begin simply—and briefly—the first few days, even weeks. The simpler, the better. Simple and direct prayers, at this juncture, will help keep *you* simple and direct. Long, complicated prayers at this point will merely confuse you; avoid them.

There are three prayers at the beginning. The first two will probably come easily. The first is, *"O God, help me,"* or *"Help someone I love."* The key here is to be specific, simple, and direct: "Help me get better...control my temper...find a job...meet this test...keep calm inside...or whatever. Help me." Or, "Help this person...."

The second is, *"O God, forgive me."* The key here is the same—be specific, simple, and direct. "O God, I am sorry I spoke in anger...did not speak in courage...was jealous...drank too much the night before last...was impatient with the children...gossiped about the boss...kicked the dog...or whatever. Forgive me."

Those are the two obvious first steps in prayer. The third, though perhaps less obvious in the beginning, is in the long run even more important. It is, *"O God, thank you."* Here you withdraw attention from yourself and direct it toward God. The key is the same—be specific, simple, and direct. "O God, thank you for my wife...my life...my health...my job...my brains...my friend John...or whatever. Thank you."

So now the preliminaries are over and we can proceed. This is where you are, so be yourself and begin where you are. And remember: *This is where God has brought you.* You can do no better now than to say: *"O God, help me.... Forgive me for.... Thank you for...."*

CHAPTER 3

Clearing the Ground

The foundation stones of prayer are the prayers you say. The base on which the life of prayer is built is simply "saying your prayers"—regularly, devotedly, and intelligently. This is the support on which all further prayer rests. So it is important to get the foundation secure. To use the figure of constructing a house, this chapter will be devoted to clearing the ground for the foundation stones. The preliminary matters to be dealt with are three.

WHEN TO PRAY

It makes no difference when you pray. Pray whenever you like. But once having chosen a time, stick to it.

There are many pressures on your time. All kinds of important matters crowd in and make demands. If you do not make time for God, you will become so busy with other concerns that you will give God no time at all. We make time for what is truly important to us; if you give to God only the time left after you have done everything else, you will spend no time at all with God, for there will be no "left over" time. So take time—any time—and keep it.

Some people pray best early in the morning, before they are involved in all the events of the day; others pray best at night, when the world has quieted down. Some pray on subways and buses, others during their lunch hours, and some on their way home from work.

There is no rule, but for most people, the best time for quiet (and quiet is your best companion for conversation with God) is in the morning when you can offer to God the events of the day that stretch before you, and in the evening when you can review those events in God's presence, commending them and yourself to God for the night.

The morning is quiet because you have not become involved in the day and are fresh; nighttime is good because you can open the levels of your consciousness to God for him to dwell there as you sleep. But do not leave all your prayer to the end of the day—else, tired, you fall asleep before prayer is done. Morning is the time for work in prayer, evening for rest in prayer.

WHERE TO PRAY

The principle here is the same: pray anywhere you like, but having chosen a place, make it your habitual place of prayer. Jesus recommended a closet to his disciples (Matthew 6:6). If you have a big enough closet, you need look no further. If not, find a place that has the virtue of closets: privacy. You need to be alone with God, where you can say what you want, in any way you want, and where you will be neither overheard nor interrupted. A familiar, secluded place is best. When traveling, Jesus often sought out a lonely spot nearby (Mark 1:35, 6:31; Luke 4:42). While a busy public place may not be ideal, such a place can become your prayer chamber if you can quiet your mind so that nearby noises do not distract you.

A place in your home (even if not your closet) is often best. It could be as simple a place as your armchair. You may set a favorite religious picture or cross before you, or a burning candle, together with devotional books you find helpful. The other natural place for private prayer is a church. Perhaps you can stop in during the day, either going to or coming from work. This is a house of prayer which already provides a devotional atmosphere, not only because of its architecture, but because faithful people have offered prayers there for many years. You can meet God most easily in his house.

In any case, select a place of privacy and go there every day to talk with God. Your prayers and God's presence will soon make it a holy place.

How to Pray

People assume various postures when praying. One man reports that he prays best while lying on the sand at the shore. Another writes that he prays best leaning back in his chair with his feet on his desk. Ignatius of Loyola recommends standing to say the Lord's Prayer and then advancing a step and kneeling to continue one's prayers. "If I find what I desire when kneeling," he writes, "I do not change to another position."

The point is that you can pray standing, sitting, kneeling, or lying down. Use whatever position is most convenient to you. The only rule is to be as natural as you can. You may find help, however, in the traditional custom of standing for thanksgiving and adoration, kneeling for confession and intercession, and sitting for meditation.

Your words should be simple and direct. They should be *your* words. Using your own words will make the prayers *your* prayers, a direct personal conversation between you and God. So speak naturally and easily as you would to a friend. Use the words that rise most simply to your lips. Don't worry about eloquence of expression. And let your prayers at the beginning revolve around the three points we discussed in the last chapter: "God, please help.... I am sorry.... I thank you."

You may soon find that you need help in your prayers, that you have said everything you think you have to say. You will begin to repeat yourself and may grow bored with prayer, afraid you are getting bogged down.

This is the time to turn for help to the prayers of other people. Written prayers from classical sources can spur our own prayers by expressing concerns we had not recognized or acknowledged. *The Book of Common Prayer* is a ready resource, and Forward Movement, Morehouse, and Church Publishing offer a number of prayer collections for every need and occasion. Most religious bookstores also offer collections of prayers. Praying the text of a hymn can also be helpful.

To whatever source you turn, *make these prayers your own.* Do not just read them, but take them into yourself and remake them, giving your imagination free rein as the words filter through your soul. As written prayers give you material and direction, they become your own.

Here, for example, is a traditional prayer, based on some words from the prophet Isaiah:

> O God of peace, who hast taught us that in returning and rest we shall be saved, in quietness and in confidence shall be our strength: By the might of thy Spirit lift us, we pray thee, to thy presence, where we may be still and know that thou art God; through Jesus Christ our Lord. Amen. (*The Book of Common Prayer,* 832)

Make this your own prayer by saying *slowly:*

> O God of peace, who has taught *me* that in returning and rest *I* shall be saved, in quietness and in confidence shall be *my* strength: By the might of thy Spirit lift *me,* I pray thee, to thy pres-

ence, where *I* may be still and know that thou art God; through Jesus Christ *my* Lord.

One source of material is especially rich for private prayer. The honesty of the biblical Book of Psalms has already been mentioned. These prayers were offered to God by people who were angry, happy, guilty, sensual, thankful, trusting, suspicious, despairing, loving, and hateful. Nothing is glossed over. The psalms are wonderful prayers to make your own. They offer a supply of prayer material you can never exhaust, and to become familiar with them will strengthen, deepen, and enrich your own prayers. Listen to yourself as you read them aloud slowly, making them your own.

Here are some suggested psalms with which to begin:

🦋 *Praise:* Psalms 103, 104, and 118

🦋 *Confession:* Psalm 51

🦋 *Help:* Psalms 31, 102, and 130

🦋 *Confidence:* Psalms 23 and 91.

You can make the psalms and other prayers your own by slowly and deliberately translating the words into your own words. This helps you express and direct toward God every thought and movement of your heart. This is personal prayer.

So much, then, for clearing the ground. This begins with the regular saying of your prayers, as often as possible in the same place. Use your own words as naturally as you can. When you need help, turn to the prayers of others and make them your own. This will prepare the way for laying the foundation.

CHAPTER 4

The Foundation Stones of Prayer

Having cleared the ground to lay the foundation, let us look at the foundation stones themselves. These are the five basic kinds of prayer. Like all good foundations, they are largely hidden from sight. As you quietly put these stones in place by regularly "saying your prayers," you make it possible later to build the proper structure for your soul.

THE PRAYER OF ADORATION

To adore God is to say, "God, I love you." It is the most important single prayer we can offer.

Your immediate reaction may be: "But I can't honestly say I love God. I'm not even sure I like him. Besides, I've only just begun to know him." Don't worry about that. You don't have to love God when you begin. Few people do—just as few couples fall in love at first sight. But if you pay attention to God, in time you will grow to love him, because God is lovable; indeed, God *is* love (1 John 4). God will help you to love him. The desire to love God may be all you have at present, and that desire is at the heart of your relationship with God. That is a form of adoration and it will bring richness and strength to your prayers.

To ask *why* we should love God is like asking a lover why he adores his beloved. His only answer can be, "Because she *is.*" So we love God not because God has helped us, answered our prayers, forgiven us our sin, or for any other gift given to us. We love God simply because God is God and we are his creatures. The prayer of adoration is to thank God for God!

As we saw in the opening chapter, God is a Person who is perfect love. God is the source of all love. All the fragmentary bits of loveliness and holiness that we know come from God and are gathered up in him.

A constant flow of love wells up in God's heart and is poured out on his creation in holiness and beauty. Only because of his love does God create and sustain the universe moment to moment. For those who see with the eyes of faith, the whole world shows forth God's glory: from the bursting forth of buds in the beauty of springtime to the love that causes someone to lay down his life for a friend. All life is surrounded and supported by God's perfect love around and above, beneath and within. We live and move and have our being in God. He is the beginning and the ending of your life and all lives. He is the be-all and end-all, from everlasting to everlasting. God, and his holiness, beauty, and love which surround us, are eternal. The prayer of adoration before such grandeur is a simple and holy one: "I love you."

A helpful but inadequate analogy, already referred to, is that of a human lover and his beloved. Lovers rest in one another, not for what they receive, but simply because the beloved other *is*. They do not beg each other or try to change each other. They may indeed use no words at all. They are content simply to *be* with each other, to adore, to will perfect love toward each other, to be whole in each other, to murmur sweet nothings. So you can adore God—through prayers, words, moods, wishes. You will not understand everything God does, or even like it. How many lovers understand and like everything their beloved does?

To adore God is to be content that God *is*, and as far as possible to rest in him. It is simply to gaze upon him and perhaps to say nothing more than a word or so: "God." "Love." "Holy." Or to say nothing at all. It is to know that the love which encompasses the universe, which flows forth as sacrifice for the beloved, encompasses you and dwells within your heart. This is holiness. And your adoring response is, "God, I love you."

The question to begin with is not "Do you love God?" but "Do you *want* to love God?" If you *want* to, you have expressed the deepest longing of the human heart. This is the response of the adoring heart.

Francis of Assisi is reported to have prayed once, "O God, help me to *want* to love you." If you can make this your prayer, you have adored God: *"O God, help me to want to love you. O God, I love you."*

THE PRAYER OF THANKSGIVING

As the prayer of adoration is to love God for himself, the prayer of thanksgiving is to thank him for what he does. It is to say, "God, I thank you for. . . ." This is the second most important prayer a person can make to God.

We have already discussed in chapter 2 the ways a prayer of thankfulness can begin. You take all the good things in your life for which you are not responsible and thank God for them.

Your attention is then directed away from yourself—your needs, problems, sins, and all the rest of it—and outward toward God. To thank God for his gifts is to break the shell we build around ourselves for protection from the blows of life. It puts the stamp of thankfulness on our relationship with God because we now concentrate on the *good* things that come from a *good* God who loves us.

Constant, consistent, day-by-day thanksgiving also helps us become joyous and thankful persons. Our response to God determines the kind of people we become. Hence the importance of thanksgiving. If you want to become a joyful person, begin by thanking God.

Start by *counting your blessings:* friends, family, love, health, work to do, tastes, sights, memories, dreams, favorite books and pieces of music and art, and all the rest. Be specific—thank God not merely for family, but for Henry and Suzanne; not just for food, but for rolled oats and figs and cheese omelettes; not just for things to read, but for Samuel Johnson, your favorite sports columnist, and your mother's recipe cards. List as many blessings as you can think of, even the lowliest blessings. Use a second and third page. You cannot expect too much from God or trust him too much as the author of everything good in your life.

Your next step is to *accept your adversities*. This is not the place to discuss that most difficult question, why a good and loving God permits so much wrong in the world. We shall consider that later. Here we are concerned not with philosophical perplexities, but with practicalities. Evil does happen; adversities do come. When you have done everything in your power to overcome them and they still remain, what do you do with them?

You *accept* them, knowing that God permits them so that through them you may turn to him. God is in charge and has purposes and means we do not now know, but we *trust* that even in adversity God draws us closer to him and gives us his blessing.

One of the great eighteenth-century men of prayer, William Law, wrote: "If anyone would tell you the shortest, surest way to all happiness and all perfection, he must tell you to make a rule to yourself to thank and praise God for everything that happens to you. For it is certain that whatever seeming calamity happens to you, if you thank and praise God for it, you turn it into a blessing."

The true saint, Law comments, "is not he who prays most, or fasts most, . . . who gives most alms or is most eminent for temperance . . . or justice; but it is he who is always thankful to God, who wills everything that God wills, who receives everything as an instance of God's goodness, and has a heart always ready to praise God for it."

The key to the prayer of thanksgiving is to take more and more of life's events—the good and the bad—into yourself as either directly from the hand of God or as having occurred with God's knowledge. It is to see in everything something of the movement of his Spirit and to realize that in every moment of our lives God wills for us perfect love, peace, and joy. God's love embraces everything that happens to us. We see this most dramatically in that act where evil did its worst—the death of God's own Son.

And now two words of warning. This does not mean we thank God for the evil in the world. Only a misguided soul would say, "Thank you, God, that I am so miserable." But we do thank God that we can receive evil as coming from within God's loving concern for us. That is why God permits it. You can turn a calamity into a blessing by thanking and praising God in the midst of it.

Nor are we to grow complacent about evil merely because we have learned to accept it in our own lives as a stepping-stone to God. We are to fight evil as fiercely as we can, in all its forms—in sickness, injustice, discrimination, poverty, oppression, war, and in every other form—just as God himself contends against evil. You are counted God's friend when you join him to battle against evil both within your soul and in the world around you.

These first two prayers of adoration and thanksgiving are closely related. You thank God for what he does in order to thank him for who he is. And as you love him for himself you see more and more his loving-kindness toward you in all the events of your life.

You can do no better than to begin now with these prayers, for which you will find no ending: *"O God, I love you. O God, I thank you for...."*

THE PRAYER OF CONFESSION

If you have ever had a disagreement with a friend or spouse, you know the reason for the prayer of confession. When you have argued with someone, you become separated.

This separation grows worse and worse until somebody says the healing words, *"I am sorry."* Once these words are spoken—honestly—the separation ends and reconciliation begins. The willingness to sacrifice a bit of ego, to confess that we are wrong, is the key to restoring a full, loving, creative relationship among friends or lovers.

As soon as we begin to acknowledge God, we recognize that we are separated from him. Indeed, our first awareness of God often comes when we realize we are separated from him and that we are not meant to be. Somehow something has gone wrong. That close friendship or union that lovers intend for each other and that God intends for us with him has been broken. What is more, we suspect at first (and positively know later on) that the fault is ours, that we have run away from God. God never runs away from us.

The key to reconciliation with God, as with a friend or lover, is to say, "I am sorry." As we turn in honest contrition, we discover that God has been waiting for us, eager to restore us to a *rightful* relationship with him. He is, in fact, more ready to forgive us than we are to ask. He urges and persuades us by every possible means until finally we recognize that we *are* separated from him, that it *is* our fault, and so say, "I am sorry." Then God begins to have his loving way with us.

If you ever disobeyed your parents as a child, suffered in your separation from them, then said "I am sorry" and were welcomed back into the bosom of your family, you know that this "confession" is what your parents wanted. They probably did everything they could to bring you to that point, to help you, wanting you back within the family. So it is with God. He does all he can to bring us to say "I am sorry," and rejoices when he welcomes us back into our rightful relationship with him.

We therefore tell God that we are sorry for what we have left undone that we ought to have done, and for what we have done that we ought not to have done. This is the general principle, but we must now translate it into practical terms.

And so we come to sin, an old but still important word. Sin is the condition of separation from God, and anything that creates or deepens that separation we call a sin. There are sins of the flesh and there are sins of the spirit. Though the former are more obvious, the latter are more deadly. It is easy to recognize the sinner who eats too much, gets drunk, and commits sexual immoralities. Anger, jealously, and pride, however, often lurk within the human heart and go unrecognized. Even in our own lives, we are more aware of sins of the flesh than of sins of the spirit embedded deep within us.

Some well-intentioned Christians have misunderstood the root of sin to be the human body and fleshly passions. This is completely untrue. The human body is good, because God made it. But how do we *use* our bodies? That is the question. If we use them only for self-indulgence, that is an expression of our sin, our separation from God. If we use them to express our love and concern for others, we avoid sin and are drawn back to God. The heart of the matter is our *choice*: do we choose for ourselves or for another?

This distinction between sins of the flesh and of the spirit is important because in trying to overcome the former we can easily succumb to the latter. Suppose you eat too much. You recognize that as a sin, confess it, and try to overcome it. You succeed and develop a moderate appetite. Then at a luncheon one day you are seated next to someone who eats as much as you once did. You say to yourself, "I am a better person than she is because I control my eating." That is pride, a spiritual sin worse than gluttony. Or you may say to yourself, "There but for the grace of God go I." This would be an act of humility and a great advance in spiritual maturity. But should you then proceed to think, "How marvelous of me to be so humble!" you would be taking pride in your humility, which is worse than taking pride in your moderate appetite. You see how closely interwoven are sins of the flesh and sins of the spirit!

Even these distinctions, however, do not fully comprehend sin and our separation from God. When we speak of sin, we usually refer to acts, either committed outwardly or suppressed inwardly. But an even deeper separation colors all our thoughts and actions. We usually look at life in terms of our wants and feelings. We see what is (or what we think is) good for us. We then try to make our good *the* good for everyone. This is true of all of us. We make our opinions into a universal standard. This keeps us from getting closer to God and to one another. And it is the root of the problem.

Even when we know this is where the trouble lies, we may not know how we got into this fix. We feel guilty, but however much we may search our hearts, we find no reason for this guilt. This is why we sometimes cry, with the psalmist, "Cleanse me from my secret faults" (Psalm 19:12, BCP). Deep down, we know we are responsible for our separation from God and from one another.

This fact of separation is called "original sin." It refers to this separation that all people share, planting within us a bias in our own favor and causing us to choose what pleases us rather than what pleases God or others. We put ourselves, rather than God, at the center of life. From this basic fact of separation arise all our particular sins, whether of the flesh or of the spirit.

Now we come to the heart of the Christian faith: the conviction that our separation from God has been overcome. God has come over to our side, joined himself to us, in the person of his Son, Jesus Christ. Through our union with Christ, God has made a way for us to get right with him. Though we may not always *feel* right, as Christians we know that we *are* right—because of what God has done for us in Christ.

To confess our sin, then, is to acknowledge that we are separated from God and cannot overcome that separation by ourselves. No amount of effort, no number of good deeds will bring us back to God. We say, "I am sorry," and as Christians we accept Christ as *the* one who overcomes the separation for us. After this confession, we proceed to thank God for this gift, his Son Jesus Christ. Through Christ we are reconciled to God, welcomed, accepted, and made one with a forgiving Father.

This is the framework within which we confess our sins to God, sins both of the flesh and of the spirit. Although we rightly tell the people we have wronged that we are sorry, sin is essentially a willful separation from God. With the psalmist we cry, "Against you only have I sinned and done what is evil in your sight" (Psalm 51:4, BCP). All sin is against God, and God sees us, even if we hurt no one and no one catches us.

When our conscience tells us we have sinned, we confess it to God. Moreover, as we draw closer to God, our conscience becomes more sensitive and our ideas of right and wrong change. A man may begin by recognizing only that God wants him to stop beating his wife, but he gradually discovers that God wants him to seek his wife's happiness in every way. Higher and higher standards of behavior are revealed to us as we draw closer to God. And at the same time we see more clearly how far short we fall of the life God desires for us. This is why a saint, who ascends to the highest levels of personal behavior, has been defined as one who sins less and less and confesses more and more.

Three more points about confession may help avoid confusion.

1. Temptation is not sin.
Do not feel guilty because temptations come your way. We live in a world with many opportunities to sin. Images and pictures flash across our minds and tempt us, often with no external cause. There is no sin in that. Sin is in *consenting* to them. Sin has to do with the will.

Do you *will* to commit the sin which tempts you? Only if you consent to it do you sin. A modern version of an illustration by William James may illustrate this (with apologies to James and to all taxi drivers). When you leave a railway train and stand on the platform where taxis are waiting, you hear each driver yelling: "Taxi! Taxi!" These are the temptations that come to us. We are at that moment free of them. Only when we deliberately choose a taxi and ride off in it, either to our destination or to our destruction, do we consent to a temptation. The sin lies in the choice we make, not in the temptation itself.

2. Private confession helps many people.

Private confession takes place when we tell God, in the presence of a priest, how we have sinned and that we are sorry. We are then assured of God's pardon by the words of absolution spoken by the priest. This is an important means of grace for people who cannot quiet their consciences by confessing alone to God.

It is God and only God who forgives sin. God hears the prayers of all who turn to him in trust and repentance. But actually reciting one's sins before God's duly ordained representative and hearing the words of absolution brings a sense of forgiveness that is often not otherwise given. Searching deliberately for the specific sins to confess and then stating them aloud is often helpful, as is hearing the strengthening words of absolution from the priest.

The purpose of private confession is to remove your sense of guilt and help you capture the joy that comes with the assurance that you are forgiven. Not everyone needs it, but if your conscience is not quieted by confessing directly to God, private confession to a priest may bring grace to your life. And the act of confessing itself is an act of humility.

3. Concentrate on Christ, not on yourself.
It is right to be concerned about our sins; it is wrong to be obsessed by them.

The best direction for our eyes is outward toward Christ, not inward toward ourselves. If we look at Christ long and seriously enough, he will reveal to us the sins he want us to confess. In his light our sins will be made apparent to us, as he wishes us to know them. Try confessing your sins by envisioning Christ actually seated beside you. But having done that, do not go on burrowing around in the murky depths of your soul, stirring the waters, fascinated more and more by your search for sins. Rather, lift up your heart and look at him who would draw you to himself. It is in his light that we see into the darkness of our hearts.

A traditional devotional exercise that has helped many through the centuries is to picture Christ on the cross. Then kneel before him and say:

O Christ, you have died for me.
What have I done for you?

From this kind of relationship will come an inner conviction of what we ought to confess.

THE PRAYER OF INTERCESSION

We have thus far been concerned with prayer as personal conversation between ourselves and God. Now we turn to prayer that has to do with others. This is called intercessory prayer.

To pray for other people is a natural human instinct. We bring the needs and concerns of others to God and ask him to help them, just as a child would bring the needs of her brothers and sisters to the attention of her parents. If the parent agrees with the request, he or she will answer the petition.

You will have to be very patient at times. God's eternal viewpoint is not the same as our limited viewpoint. Nor are we the first to be impatient with God—many of the psalms contain requests that God "hasten" or "hurry up" and do something. You may also have to readjust your ideas of what the people you pray for actually need, again because our viewpoint is not God's viewpoint. You can be certain, though, that God wants you to pray for others and that he will, in one way or another, in his own time, and in the *best* way, answer your prayer.

We are surrounded by *mystery*. How God responds to prayer is part of that mystery. Why do some prayers appear to be answered immediately and just as we hoped, while others seemingly are not answered for years, and then in ways we do not expect or want? And why are some prayers not, at least from our perspective, answered at all? Nowhere is the mystery in which our lives are steeped more apparent than when we wrestle with birth and beginning, death and ending, suffering and sin. It does no good to pretend to see clearly when in fact we see through a glass darkly.

But we can also affirm *certainty* within the mystery surrounding intercessory prayer. When we pray, some things happen that would not otherwise have happened. Perhaps they occur as we expect, perhaps not. But when we pray, we can be certain, based on evidence observed as well as on faith, that things are taking place because of our prayer. William Temple is reported to have said, "When you stop praying, coincidences stop." This is perhaps as good a proof of intercessory prayer as there is. And you can prove it yourself: when you pray persistently for a person, notice the coincidences that begin to occur. (C. S. Lewis has written an insightful essay on this entitled "The Efficacy of Prayer," available as a tract from Forward Movement Publications.)

When we pray for others, then, we do so humbly, because we know we are surrounded by mystery and do not have all the answers. We also, however, pray with confidence because of our certainty that God does have the answers. So let us turn to consider the best way to pray for people and causes.

Two principles underlie all intercessory prayer. The first is to *be expectant, specific, and persistent.* Expect the very best to happen to the person for whom you pray. Be confident of the best; trust God to bring it to pass. If you are praying for a sick person to get well, for example, expect healing. Picture the person in your mind as already healed and thank God for bringing it about. One reason many prayers seem to go unanswered is that we expect so little of prayer. When you pray, expect the best.

Pray specifically. Mention people by name and state their specific needs. To pray for people in large groups— the poor, the church, our country—is helpful but inadequate. Also pray for individual persons in a personal way and do not hesitate to pray for what you believe they need. To be sure, you may discover that their actual needs differ from their apparent needs, and your understanding will change and deepen. A vague, general prayer, however, is unsubstantial. It is more helpful to be concrete and to pray specifically for healing, a job, reconciliation, money, or whatever you think the need is.

Persistence in prayer calls for patience. It also means claiming from God what we as Christians have a right to expect. God's eternity is not the same as our time. We sometimes grow impatient and give up because God appears to work so slowly. Remember that his grace has all of eternity to accomplish its ends and that all our prayers will be answered, even if it be on the other side of the grave. But even in the brief time given us on this side, patient, persistent prayer has power and brings forth more fruit than prayers that are impetuous and cursory.

Also remember that as God's children, we can expect certain things from him. God has promised never to forsake us and always to forgive. We need never be afraid or feel alone. God has adopted us through Christ as his children, promising us the comfort and power of his Spirit. All that a human father would do for his children, God will do for us—and more. We have a right, therefore, to insist on these promises and to pray persistently for God's children whose needs we know and whom we bring before him. And if he seems to pay no attention, it may be that only to our persistent prayer will he reply.

The second principle of intercessory prayer is that *the best prayer is Christ's prayer: Thy will be done.* This was the prayer Christ offered to God in the Garden of Gethsemane on the night in which he was betrayed. He asked God very specifically to take away the suffering that loomed before him the next day. Suffering was not what *he* wanted. Yet Christ knew that what *God* wanted would in the long run be best for his work, for the world, and for himself. Therefore, he concluded his prayer: "*Thy will be done.*"

It is this prayer of Christ's that makes intercessory prayer Christian prayer. When all our prayers are rooted in our desire that God's will be done in those for whom we pray, we are praying *in Jesus' name.* These prayers are already answered—though they may not be answered in our way. We may not understand how they should be answered. Sooner or later, though, we discover that suffering is embedded in the universe and cannot be avoided. No magic word will turn it aside. Sometimes it is only through suffering that God's will can be done. Given the nature of the world and our sin, some suffering is inescapable. It should not surprise us, therefore, that when we look into the mystery of praying for others, we discover that at the heart of it is the cross. Christ's prayer that God's will be done was answered in and through his suffering. He who was without sin suffered for all others. This was intercession at its highest. God's will was accomplished only by that intercession. It meant suffering, but it was God's way, and it was the best way. It is the way of the cross.

One final thought. The One we address in prayer loves those for whom we pray more than we love them. He is infinitely wiser than we and will do for them greater things than we can ever pray for. However dark and hopeless things may appear to us, God has the will and the power to do what is best. Though mystery surrounds us, we can be certain that at its heart is the love of God and that God will do for all his children all that a human parent would do—and infinitely more.

THE PRAYER OF PETITION

God wants us to bring our own needs to him as well as those of others. Prayer for ourselves is called petitionary prayer. All that has been said about intercessory prayer can also be said of petitionary prayer. Prayer for ourselves can even be seen as an extension of our prayer for others. The same principles underlie both.

Most people begin by asking God to help them in specific and concrete ways. It is only natural to want God to meet our needs as we perceive them. So we tell him we need a better job, or more money, or deeper understanding from those around us, or help out of a difficulty, whatever we think we need. This is the normal way to begin.

We end, however, by asking God to help us as *he* sees fit, to meet our needs not as we see them, but as God sees them. Our perfect prayer, for ourselves as for others, is Christ's prayer: "Not my will but yours be done" (Luke 22:42). For Jesus, this meant the cross. For us, too, the cross may be the only way God's will can be done in us.

Do not be surprised, then, to discover that your prayers are not answered exactly as you might wish. Be prepared for a denial of your terms so that you may come to understand God's terms. His wise refusals of what we want help us know what he wants; and when we honestly come to want for ourselves what God wants, we have attained the heights of petitionary prayer. This may mean accepting suffering rather than avoiding it, but we are not discouraged, for with acceptance comes the strength to bear it well. This is the way of the cross. As with our prayers for others, this is God's way and it is the best way.

Our prayers of petition, then, will always be expectant, open, and confident. We shall be surprised at nothing and prepared for everything as God answers our prayer. Confident that his answers are always the best answers, we trust him to provide those answers in his own way and in his own time. If his will can be done only through our bearing some suffering, we rejoice as he gives us strength to bear our cross. For us as for Christ, this is entrance into the peace that comes from doing God's will, the peace that passes understanding. This peace, however it comes to us, is the ultimate answer to our prayer of petition. If we ask for it, it will surely be given to us, for God is as gracious to us as any human father toward his children—and infinitely more so.

These then are the five foundation stones of prayer. All that is later built into the life of prayer rests upon these foundation stones. You build a firm foundation for your prayer life by incorporating each of the five stones into it, omitting none.

They are the five responses you make to God who has begun to touch you. Indeed, it is better to say that they are the five ways God responds through you, for it is he who inspires you to pray. Think, then, of your prayers as God's prayers, of your desire to pray as God already inspiring you, for, as Paul says, "it is God who is at work in you, enabling you both to will and to work for his good pleasure" (Philippians 2:13).

God is helping you to build a broad, strong foundation. Now say: *"O God, I love you. I thank you for.... I am sorry for.... Please help Jane...John...us...me.... Not my will, but yours be done."*

CHAPTER 5

The House That Prayer Builds

Let us now assume that the ground has been cleared and the foundation stones laid. You have begun to say your prayers regularly and wish to get on with constructing your house. The house that prayer builds is your soul. By the word *soul* we mean the total response of your whole personality to God, what is completely "you" in relation to God. This chapter is about the soul, the general structure and design you can expect your house to take as you advance beyond merely "saying your prayers."

Many people think saying their prayers is all there is to prayer. Some never advance beyond reciting short memorized prayers like "Now I lay me down to sleep." Having said such prayers for years, they grow discouraged. Bored with a dull routine, they think there is nothing more and so give up even saying their prayers.

Saying our prayers is important, but there is more to prayer. This is the new house to be built on the foundation laid out in the last chapter.

The house that prayer builds has three stories. We shall discuss them one at a time, though in practice they are not separated so sharply—sometimes you cannot separate them at all. The three kinds of prayer are different but they blend so that it is often hard to see where one leaves off and the other begins. The three kinds of prayer are:

- Prayers that you *think*
- Prayers that you *feel*
- Prayers that you *will*.

We shall look at each in turn, but remember that all three are involved to some degree in every prayer. You cannot *think* a prayer without *feeling* something because you have *willed* it.

PRAYERS THAT YOU THINK

To *think* a prayer is to direct your mind toward God, to use your intelligence consciously in God's presence. This is sometimes called *meditation*. As vocal prayer is saying your prayers, so meditation is *thinking* your prayers. You make the fullest possible use of your intellect to understand some part of the truth of God. To worship God fully with your mind is the purpose of prayers that you think.

There is nothing mysterious or difficult about such prayers. If you have ever thought about God at all, you have meditated on him. What is God like? Why did he begin the world? How can a loving God permit such evil to triumph in his world? If you have ever pondered such questions, you have meditated upon God.

To think your prayers deliberately is to wrestle with understanding God's actions. It is to recognize that as we think, so we are, and to attempt to "think God's thoughts after him." This means concentrating on some aspect of God or his activity until you begin to understand it, and then to apply it to your life.

In meditating on the power of God, for example, you can think through the act of creation as a continuing, sustaining act on the part of God; relate this to the problems of atomic power, environmental destruction, and global warming; consider how we can appropriate God's power to support rather than destroy creation; and resolve to use what power God has given us for God's creative purposes. Or you can meditate on the loveliness of God seen in a beautiful sunset, with its changing colors forming a canopy over the sky, sheltering and protecting you, and know yourself to rest under the cover of God's wing. Or you can watch the rain sink into the parched earth and think of how this is like God's love poured on us. This is to think a prayer.

You can meditate on anything, from the mystery of the vast heavens to the sparrow that falls to the ground, still within God's loving care. When you use your mind to ponder God, his relationship to the world of nature and our lives, you are *thinking* prayers. Whatever helps you perceive, apply, and inwardly digest the reasons for the actions of God is to be welcomed and fed upon. This will not be the same for everyone. Respond in whatever way God seems to be leading you, and meditate on any truth that seems to apply to you.

It is no accident, of course, that most people who take meditation seriously are drawn to the Bible. Since God has shown himself most fully in the history of the Jews over the centuries, and particularly in the life of one Jew, Jesus of Nazareth, it is natural that the subjects for meditation often come from the Bible. Here is the record of what God has done with his people and in his Son. By staying close to the Bible, we stay close to the source of Christian thought and life.

The Bible tells us how God acts. God judges all human sin, regardless of who we are, and calls us to understand him more deeply, no matter how advanced we think we are. Keep this picture before you. Meditate on God's action, especially in Jesus Christ. Remember that you are judged by God because you are still involved in sin, and that however advanced in the spiritual life you may be, you still fall short of the goal disclosed in Jesus Christ. Without this objective standard, we tend to judge ourselves by our own values; we do not seek to think God's thoughts, but imagine that God is thinking our thoughts. The straightforward biblical account of God shown in Jesus Christ is the best protection against our own subjectivism.

If you have ever read a Bible story and tried to figure out what it means and apply it to yourself, you have already meditated. Countless boys, for example, have read the story of David and Goliath, identified with David, and perhaps been inspired to act courageously when faced with a bully at school. If they then related their courage to God who inspires them, as he inspired David, they made an even better meditation.

Our purpose is to meditate in more defined and specific ways than we often do in casual meditations, to think systematically on biblical scenes. Only through intelligent meditation is an intimate, personal relationship with God possible. It marks a great step forward in the life of prayer. Let us now examine a method for the devotional use of the Bible that will enable us intelligently to approach a biblical scene so that we may appropriate it for our lives. These are three suggested steps:

1. *Picture* a biblical scene.

2. *Ponder* its meaning.

3. *Promise* God something as a result.

1. Picture a biblical scene.

To *picture* an episode or scene from the Bible as vividly as possible is the important first step. This method of entering into a biblical scene was developed by Ignatius of Loyola in the sixteenth century. Use your intellect and all your senses so that the scene becomes alive, intimate, and personal. Picture yourself there. What is the weather? What time of day is it? Use all the five senses: hear the shouts and listen to the voices, smell the flowers and the people, touch the rough stones, taste the blade of grass, gaze into the faces of the people. Are the faces joyful, angry, agitated, bored, threatened, curious? What expression does your face bear? What is your role in the scene? Are you an observer, standing on the fringe of the crowd, hesitant to move to the center, or are you a participant, perhaps the one approaching and questioning

Jesus? Or possibly the one approached, the one being questioned? What are you thinking, saying, doing there?

Here, for example, is an imaginative description of the scene where Simon Peter meets Jesus for the first time (Mark 1:16–20). Imagine that you are Peter, relating this incident many years later to people who had never known Jesus.

"I shall never forget," you say, "the day I threw in my lot with him. I was a fisherman, an ordinary, everyday kind of fisherman, like my father before me. I was uncouth, with my share of sins and maybe a bit more. One day my partners, James and John, and I had spent all morning patrolling our nets. Since we hadn't caught even a minnow all night long, we took the nets in and were washing them on some rocks.

"A crowd of people appeared on the shore—forty or fifty of them—with a young man at their head. As they drew near, the young man asked to sit in my boat while he talked to these people. I said I'd help him. While I held the boat, he got in and sat in the stern. I took up the oars and shoved off a little distance from the shore, and the people gathered on the bank in a little semicircle. For about half an hour he talked to them about God and his kingdom, and how they could trust God within his kingdom. I wasn't paying much attention, but I was struck by the way he talked. He seemed to know what he was talking about, almost as if he had some kind of inside information about God and his kingdom.

"When he finished, he blessed them, and as they walked off, he turned to me and said, 'Simon, let's go out fishing.' 'Sorry, Rabbi,' I said, 'but there are no fish today.' 'Let's go see,' he said. I decided to humor him. So I rowed out, tossed over a net, and to my astonishment, pulled it in full. I dumped it out in the bottom of the boat and it was flooded with fish flapping around. Then I threw over another net, and it was so heavy with fish that I couldn't pull it in, so I called for my partners. James and John came alongside in another boat. I tossed them a line and we all began to pull. The load was so heavy that both boats began to ship water and we started to go under, with fish flapping all around us.

"I looked at Jesus. He was sitting still in the stern. I had the thought that he was somehow responsible for all this. It scared me. I fell to my knees and cried, 'Sir, go away! I am a sinful man!' He put his hand on my shoulder and called me by name. He looked at me—or rather, he looked through me, beyond me. For the first time in my life I felt I was *known*. And *held*. I felt I couldn't move. I was even more frightened than before, but he said, 'Don't be afraid.' And I wasn't afraid. He would say the same thing—'Don't be afraid'—many times in the years that followed.

"We hauled in what fish we could and rowed back to shore. Then Jesus looked at us again and said, 'Follow me. From now on, you will fish for people.' He and I walked along the beach, with James and John a few steps behind. The waves lapped on the shore. I looked at them and listened to them. What was happening here? Where was I headed? But I was no longer afraid."

That is to *picture* the scene.

2. *Ponder its meaning.*
The second step is to *ponder* the scene. Think hard about it. What does it mean? What is God trying to do here? What is God trying to say to *you*?

For example, as you ponder the scene just pictured, you may encounter Jesus taking the initiative and walking into your life, just as he took the initiative and walked into Peter's life. Jesus always starts the relationship; we respond—or do not respond.

We are free to invite Jesus to sit in our boat or to tell him to get out. He never coerces, but waits upon our willing consent to welcome him into our lives. Love is always a gift which we are free to accept or reject.

Again, ponder what it means to be known. What did Peter experience when he suddenly realized he was entirely known? Very few people truly know us, or want to. How difficult it is to enter fully into the heart and mind of someone else, even those we love most deeply! Yet there is One who sees into the depths of our hearts, knows all about us, from whom we can hide nothing. It is both wonderful and terrifying to be known as Jesus knows us!

When the boat starts to sink, we are afraid. Our fear is mixed with guilt, for confronted by the holiness of Christ, we see ourselves as we truly are. Being known by Christ is the means by which we know ourselves.

Or ponder the meaning of "Be not afraid." All our anxiety, loneliness, and fear are wiped away as we know ourselves to be with One who loves us forever and will never leave us alone.

Consider that Jesus always enters our lives in the company of other people. We do not meet him alone, but always with others. At first, we know him through our parents, church school teachers, and friends. But sooner or later, we deal with Jesus alone. This usually involves a struggle, for our first impulse is to tell Jesus to go away—we must choose Jesus or our sins. But once this is settled and we understand that we are known and forgiven and there is nothing to fear, we can go on. We go about our daily living in company with others and with Jesus. And we accept our responsibility to carry Jesus into the lives of people, as he once came into our life through others. Like Peter, James, and John, we become fishers of men.

It can help to imagine the lives of biblical characters *before* the scene unfolds. What was Peter like before he met Jesus? How did he spend his free time? What was he thinking as he washed out his nets? This is to get a running start on the meditation before it actually begins. We are in any case to think, to get our minds around the incident, to *ponder.*

3. Promise God something as a result.
The final step is to *promise.* A meditation is only complete when it results in action; prayer is not prayer until some act is made. The results of our pondering need to be pinned down and made concrete. Prayer that results in no action and merely stimulates the mind and excites the emotions is not only useless but dangerous. The final step therefore is to *promise* to do something. If possible, it should be simple, definite, and practical, and the sooner done the better.

Your promise may be nearly anything: "God, I promise to invite Cynthia into my life today as Peter welcomed you into his... to try to discover and meet Henry's deepest needs... to put away this one sin... to try to come to know Susan better this day... to help anyone I meet who is afraid... to write to a lonely person."

Any biblical scene offers inexhaustible riches to those who conscientiously try to think their prayers by these three steps: to picture, to ponder, to promise. This is particularly true as you envision the scene on the hill of Calvary and think of what God has done through Christ on the cross there. Many systems of meditation have been developed and you should follow whatever system leads you most easily into natural conversation with God. What has been described here is simply one easy system that has helped many people.

PRAYERS THAT YOU FEEL

To *feel* prayers is to involve your emotions in your relationship to God. Your emotions are always engaged in some way when you think about God. As you remember God's good gifts, you *like* them and you *rejoice*. You are *ashamed* of your failures and express your *sorrow*. You *thank* God for his help and tell him of your *love*. In a time of loss you may feel *angry* at God. Fervor of spirit, depth of feeling, and the longings of your heart are part of the flesh and blood of your prayer life.

Aroused emotions and warm feelings are among the ways we respond to God. Use your emotions in your prayers just as you use your mind. Emotions bring color and richness, breadth and length, height and depth to your relationship with God. They also bring power because the emotions are a driving force more powerful than the intellect.

As you think of God, therefore, and dwell upon some aspect of who God is or what he does, let your feelings flow naturally and express themselves as they will. Add the power of your emotional drives to your mental thoughts as you respond more fully to God.

If you are meditating, for example, on the beauty of God as seen in nature, do not hesitate to pray in some such way as this: "O God, I marvel and rejoice at the colors of the sky, the movement of the seas, the blowing of the wind in the trees, and the voice of the cricket in the field. How wonderful you are, holding all that is, letting nature bring the beauty of your nature to me, and helping me lift my voice. My heart rejoices and sings in your created world!"

If your thinking has led you to dwell on the loveliness of Christ, let yourself go and speak thus with him: "O Jesus, beloved of your Father and beloved of my soul, I long for you and your goodness. I lift my heart to you. I would love you with the perfect love you have for me. Be mine, that I may be yours forevermore. O Christ, blessed are you whom I love and adore!"

Let your emotions follow your thoughts naturally. Do not try to force your emotions or strain them or make them express what you do not truly feel. Even negative emotions such as confusion and anger at God should be expressed honestly. As you meditate on God and his love for you, the inner motions of your heart will gradually become emotions of love returned to God. There is, for example, a peace from God which flows over us as we think of him as perfect peace. "Those of steadfast mind you keep in peace—in peace because they trust in you" (Isaiah 26:3). We receive such peaceful emotions as we deliberately turn our minds to God. Feelings follow thoughts.

At this point an almost imperceptible change begins to take place. You may not be aware of it at the time and may recognize it only as you look back. A husband and wife grow to love each other through successive stages, but they are aware of them only in retrospect, as when they declare, after years of marriage, "It is a miracle that we ever dared to get married, for we had then no real idea of what love was like."

Because of this gradual change in your love relationship to God, one day you discover that you are paying less attention in prayer to formal steps, external guides, and specific requests. Rather than wondering how, when, or where your prayers will be answered, you are now content simply to lay them before God, knowing that he will answer in his way and time as is best for you.

You are more and more content simply to be with God. You become aware of being *in* him. The tension or strain of "you" and "God" as two different persons in relationship is slackened. God is still distinct from you and remains so, but now you are more sensitive to God as moving within you and the people and events that touch you. It is almost as though God were in you and you in him. There is an intimacy you never knew before.

As you grow less dependent on the rules of prayer, it is as though God himself becomes your guide. You begin to trust God and to follow leadings that seem to come directly from God within you. You are content with fewer words, perhaps only single words: "God." "Love." "Blessed Jesus." "Holy One."

This kind of prayer eventually leads you to the Center. The Center seems to enfold you; externals have fallen away. The Quakers have the wonderful phrase "centering down." Here within us (yet also outside us) is the Deep, the Quiet, the Rest of the Spirit of God himself.

Now you do not move. You do not agitate. You simply *are*. God holds you in the Quiet and you rest within him as your Center. God *is*. You two, together. You feel no need to speak now, and no need to listen. You simply are in God and he is in you. You look at, contemplate, rest in each other, love each other. It is love responding to love. This is to be "prayed through." It is as though you were "inspired," "breathed through" by a Spirit coming from beyond, welling up within, and carrying you in response back to its source. God having found you, and you having responded, God has now brought you into himself—and yet you are still you.

This is a glimpse of what heaven must be: you and the whole company of souls with you in such a relation with God and each other. Here is a foretaste of the glory of being caught up, surrounded, and indwelt by the perfect love that is God. The basic reality is God—God loving you and you being loved through by him. There is above and beneath and within nothing but the all-consuming motions of love, loving perfectly and wholly and completely. And yet you remain. You are not consumed. You are still you! In heaven you are loved and able to love finally and fully and forever, for you are now at one with God and with all others so bound to him. From time to time, we feel heaven about us on earth!

But this will pass. Such an experience of ecstasy cannot remain. It may come and go in a flash, and for some people, decades or even a lifetime goes by without such an experience. If you have been given such a moment, return to your regular ways when it passes. Do not be impatient because your "mountaintop" feelings have gone, but give thanks that they have come to you and trust that they will, in God's good time, return. *Feelings* come and go; do not trust them. God remains and you remain. Trust God.

PRAYERS THAT YOU WILL

To *will* a prayer is to direct your entire self to God, no matter how you feel. This is the final and most essential prayer. It is *you* praying, the real you as your emotions are not *you*. When you have said to God, "I *will* to thank you; I *will* to love you; I *will* to submit to you," you have expressed the very heart of your relationship to God. This will is the core of your soul.

You are to trust not your feelings about God, but God himself. Whether you feel God near or far away has nothing to do with the facts. Whatever your feelings, God is where you are. Important as the emotions are for action—they provide the driving power for most actions—they are nonetheless unreliable *guides* for action. Your intellect and your will are surer guides.

Relying on feelings can be treacherous. You may, for example, feel happy one day and unhappy the next, for no apparent reason, when your actual condition has not changed. You are drawn to like some people and dislike others—again for superficial reasons. Sometimes you like people you ought to dislike and dislike those you have good reason to like. We are all subject to moods and changes of temperament, and emotional feelings can fluctuate for no rational rhyme or reason.

So it is with our feelings about God. Sometimes we feel close to God. At other times we feel apart from God. Again we feel that God does not exist at all. These feelings have *nothing* to do with the reality. Either God is or he is not. If God is, then he is where you are, precisely there, and your feelings have no bearing on it.

So do not trust your feelings as guides in your relationship with God. Feelings come and go. They are helpful when they make you "feel" near God, but nothing has changed if that feeling departs from you. Both God and you are still there, together. The real question to ask is whether you *want* God there with you. This has to do with your will, with your choices, with the most basic decisions of your life. It has to do with the real *you*.

Thus the prayers that mean the most are those that you will. This is not to say that prayers *thought* and prayers *felt* are not honest prayers. It is simply to say that when they are *willed* they become complete.

You make the greatest forward strides in prayer precisely when feelings are withdrawn and you have nothing to go on except your intellect and your will. It is then that you can decide whether you want God for himself or only for his gifts. God makes a great act of trust toward us when he takes all feelings away to enable us to trust him alone, rather than our feelings about him. This opportunity to *trust* God alone because we know we *want* him alone is a great means of grace that he gives us. So when your feelings toward God go away, thank God with your will, because that means you have advanced enough for God to trust you.

To say, "O God, I want *you*," is the great prayer of the will. Here you pray to God and hold on to the personal relationship with him not because you need to, nor because you ought to, but because you want to. It is you and God alone in the essential part of your nature—your will. And if you are not quite at that point, perhaps you can pray, "O God I *want* to want you." That is enough.

The house that prayer builds, then, is your soul. The prayer that builds this house is always threefold: thinking, feeling, and willing. Although we have separated them artificially in our discussion, they are closely intertwined. While one aspect or another will be stressed from prayer to prayer, all elements are in every prayer, and the most complete prayer includes all.

So the house is built. The foundation stones are firmly in place and made more secure day by day as your prayers of adoration, thanksgiving, confession, intercession, and petition continue to be said. The dwelling place of the soul is then constructed, with variations for individual patterns, as prayers that stress the intellect, the emotions, and the will take their proper places. This is the mansion where the soul dwells and where God is your constant companion and guest.

The building of the house of prayer that is your soul continues as long as you live. Once the house is built, the next step is to move in and make the house a home to live in. It is to this enrichment and deepening of the life of prayer that we now turn.

CHAPTER 6

Progress in Prayer

Not to advance in the spiritual life is to go back. As we grow in age, we are meant to grow in grace. But progress in prayer is not automatic. It comes only as we deliberately attend to God and develop habits of thought and action that keep God before our minds. In this chapter we shall consider ways to pay attention to God and thus come to know and love him more.

PRACTICING THE PRESENCE OF GOD

"Prayer for busy people" is the concern of this section. How does someone facing the distractions and demands of earning a living or keeping a house, with only limited time for devotional practices, gain the sense of God's presence that is necessary for progress in prayer?

The secret is to pray in and through all your busyness and activity. Let the work you do and the people you meet be themselves vehicles for your prayers. Cultivate the sense of God's presence not as something to be gained apart from your daily living, but within all the events and activities of the day.

Take *any given moment* on *any given day*. That moment, and all it contains for good or for evil, is the means by which God is trying to break into your life to communicate with you. No matter your circumstances, God is as involved in them as you are and is trying to use them to say something to you. If you are discouraged, God is concerned to give you hope; if you are guilty, he is asking you to say you are sorry so that he may forgive you; if you are frightened, he is calling you to trust in him; if you have a task, he offers you the strength to accomplish it. Whatever a given moment may hold for you, it is the means by which God comes into your life, so that you may know him more fully, love him more deeply, and serve him more ably. There is *never* a moment that is outside God's providence. You can be aware of God and respond to him moment by moment in your busyness and still go about the tasks of the day.

Another way to practice the presence of God in your daily living is to look for him in and through the *people you meet*. You can learn to see each person as bearing God to you. You see this easily in people who need you: the sick, the unhappy, the forlorn, the lonely, the poor, the rejected. It is also true of those who seem not to need you, and especially of those who do not like you. We can always ask God, "What are you trying to say to me through this person?" When someone irritates you, God may be saying, "Be patient." When someone criticizes you, God may be saying, "Think how he would judge you if he knew you as I know you." When someone you trusted betrays you, God may be saying, "Your final trust and confidence must be in me, not in people."

Your response to the person will also be your response to God. You will remain open to every human relationship and learn to treat each person as a God-bearer; God himself will come to you through these relationships. God will involve himself in your life as every person is involved. However many people may be engaged with you, God will come to you through all of them and you will have a more constant sense of his presence.

Another way you can experience God's presence is to become sensitive to his handiwork in *the world of nature*. The heavens, flowers, birds, mountains, floods, mists, meadows, sunsets, and storms all contain signs and symbols that the whole realm of nature is God's. They point to him. It is often in this natural world that people are first aware of "something more" than meets the eye, of "something other" brooding over them, of "someone else" beckoning to them, calling them onward. Perhaps quite suddenly, you may be broken in upon, touched, and lifted into another presence. You are in touch with the reality that sustains and lies behind the world of nature—God.

Such intimations are to be welcomed. You can cultivate sensitivity to these "breakings through" and put yourself in the way of them. Go again and again to wherever the beauty and awesomeness of nature makes you feel closest to God: walking along the beach at the breaking of the waves; at dusk as shadows lengthen and the world for a moment seems to stand still; beneath the stars at night; lying on the bow of a boat as it rides into the rolling sea; inhaling the fragrance of an herb garden; watching a bird light on a branch and fly off instantly. To respond by lifting your heart in thanksgiving to God is to be stirred by his Spirit and reminded that you are constantly in his presence.

Nature is not the fullest disclosure of God, but it is a true disclosure and it is where many of us begin. In time, as we respond to him, we come to understand that God is far more than an emotional experience of beauty and wonder, that he is the One shown fully in Jesus Christ. This fuller understanding comes, however, only as we respond to our best understanding of God where we begin. Once you have responded to the leading of God and been brought to his deepest manifestation in Jesus Christ, you can turn back to the world of nature and see signs of God everywhere. Having known God's love in Christ, you find and are fed by lesser manifestations of that same love in the beauty of nature. It is a sure sign of spiritual depth to see the glory of God in a rose, for example, and to praise him for it, because you have seen it most fully on the cross.

You may develop a sense of God's presence, finally, by reminding yourself that *God lives within you.* The "inner light" and the "still, small voice" testify to God. Christ is known within, and the interior life can be built on a quiet and constant inner conversation with him.

A man tells of going into a church late one afternoon. Kneeling down in the shadows there, withdrawn from the busy world, with only the quiet coming and going of others who, like him, had come to pray briefly, he was given a sense of the presence of Christ within him.

"I was gradually aware," he said, "of a presence around the altar which could not be described in terms other than those familiar, though to that moment misunderstood words: 'Real Presence.' I thought to myself, 'Christ is there.' Then my eyes fell upon a crucifix attached to the wall and I thought, 'Christ is there, too.' The people praying next to me impressed me, and it came to me, 'Christ is within them as well.' The next thought overwhelmed me: 'Christ is inside my own heart.' So I thought I should say something to him. Cautiously, I asked, 'Why don't you give me more help, Jesus?' And the reply came back immediately, 'I will when you give yourself *wholly* to me.' 'All right. Right now I give myself and all I hope to be to you.' 'Then remember that I am your friend. I am within you. I will be with you with power forever.'" This is to know Christ within. It is one way to practice the presence of God.

To summarize, busy people can pray in and through their activities as they practice the presence of God. God is present in every moment of your life. He is present in every person who deals with you. He reveals himself through nature. He is known as a living presence within you. All these ways together will help you develop a sense of God's presence, and as you respond to them, there will be no end to the increase of grace given you.

One of the masters in this art of practicing the presence of God was a retired soldier known to the world as Brother Lawrence. Near the end of his life he made this comment: "Were I a preacher, I should, above all things, preach the practice of the presence of God.... He requires no great thing of us: a little remembrance of him from time to time, a little adoration; sometimes to pray for his grace, sometimes to offer him your sufferings, and sometimes to return him thanks for the favors he has given you, and still gives you, in the midst of your troubles, and to console yourself with him the oftenest you can. Lift up your heart to him...the least little remembrance will always be acceptable to him. You need not cry very loud; he is nearer to us than we know."

A final hint: Memorize some reminders of God. Simple little sentences or prayers said frequently during the course the day will in time lift your mind constantly to God's presence. The best phrases are those you select yourself to meet your particular need, but some typical ones are these: "Glory to you, O Lord. Praise to you, O Christ. Blessed Lord Jesus. Lord Jesus Christ, have mercy on me, a sinner. You are my God and I will praise you; you are my God, I will exalt you. All things work together for good to those who love you. I can do all things through Christ who strengthens me."

READING, PRAYER GROUPS, AND RETREATS

Different Christians have, to varying degrees, found help in the life of devotion from three sources. For some they are indispensable: they undergird and strengthen the interior life and make possible an increase of grace. They are reading, prayer groups, and retreats.

Reading
Men and women who have loved God in their day have left accounts of their experiences to help us know and

love God in our day. Reading of the experiences of those who have walked with God before us is one of the great aids to progress in prayer. Although the forms of expression may differ, the knowledge and love offered to God are the same from generation to generation.

The book, of course, is the Bible. As no other book, this one has led people through the ages to feed upon the living Word of God, to be sustained and comforted and guided by him. There is no substitute for daily reading of the Bible. Use a modern translation and look for an edition with notes and introductory material. Many such Bibles are available in religious bookstores, but not all are of the highest quality. Ask your priest or pastor to suggest one. A good commentary can also be helpful, such as the long popular Daily Bible Study Series by William Barclay and the more recent *New Testament for Everyone* commentary by N. T. Wright. But remember that it is the Bible you are to digest, not the commentaries.

When reading the Bible, begin with one of the four gospels or perhaps with one of the epistles. It is better to read a small portion of scripture thoughtfully than to read a lot of scripture hurriedly. Reading a passage several times is often helpful, asking a different question each time: To whom and for what purpose was this passage originally written? What is God saying to me today through this passage? Where does it challenge me? What am I to do about it?

Next to the Bible, for Episcopalians, is *The Book of Common Prayer.* Intended for corporate worship, the Prayer Book is also a treasury of material for private devotional use. In addition to prayers for seasons of the year and events in people's lives, it contains a two-year plan for daily Bible reading, with three short passages and a psalm for each day. Many readers find it helpful to supplement their Bible reading with the meditation in *Forward Day by Day*. Each meditation is based on one of the Bible passages for that day from the Prayer Book. (*Forward Day by Day* is published quarterly and is available from Forward Movement Publications.)

Then there are the spiritual classics, which never lose their appeal. Most of these are available in inexpensive paperback editions. Here, too, use a modern translation. Among the best are these:

- *Confessions* by Augustine of Hippo (fourth century). The first (and many would say still the best) spiritual autobiography, relating the author's search for God and God's search for him.

- *Prayers and Meditations* by Anselm of Canterbury (eleventh century). A classic of personal devotion, the first work of its kind.

- *On the Love of God* by Bernard of Clairvaux (twelfth century). Sets forth a traditional pattern for the life of prayer, especially for those whose main work is prayer.

- *The Imitation of Christ* by Thomas à Kempis (fifteenth century). A Dutch monk offers a series of dialogues with Christ, maxims, and prayers.

- *The Spiritual Exercises* by Ignatius Loyola (sixteenth century). A manual for retreat leaders, including some prayers and suggestions for biblical meditation.

❧ *The Practice of the Presence of God* by Brother Lawrence (seventeenth century). A short booklet in which a single-minded lay brother tells how to experience the immediacy of God amid the day-to-day chores of life.

❧ *An Introduction to the Devout Life* by Francis de Sales (seventeenth century). Perhaps the most helpful guide to the life of devotion for busy people who must live in the world and accept responsibilities within it.

❧ *Private Devotions* by Lancelot Andrewes (seventeenth century). A program of prayer for the seven days of the week, broad in scope but specific in focus and intention.

❧ *The Pilgrim's Progress* by John Bunyan (seventeenth century). Long the most popular devotional book among English-speaking Protestants, it is an allegory of the Christian's journey through life.

❧ *Journal* by George Fox (seventeenth century). The founder of the Society of Friends (Quakers) tells the story of his life and his benevolent behavior toward all, even when maligned and persecuted.

❧ *Pensées* by Blaise Pascal (seventeenth century). A mathematician's thoughts on spiritual questions.

❧ *Abandonment to Divine Providence* by Jean Pierre de Caussade (eighteenth century). Meditations on surrendering every moment and concern to God's providential care.

❧ *A Serious Call to a Devout and Holy Life* by William Law (eighteenth century). An uncompromising call for faithful living in every aspect of life.

❧ *Journal* by John Wesley (eighteenth century). The founder of the Methodist movement relates his life of preaching and evangelism among the poor and downtrodden of Britain.

❧ *Journal* by John Woolman (eighteenth century). The autobiography of an American Quaker.

Many more recent authors have also written helpful devotional works. Among them are:

❧ *Letters to a Niece* by Friedrich von Hügel.

❧ *Concerning the Inner Life* and *The Spiritual Life* by Evelyn Underhill.

❧ *A Testament of Devotion* by Thomas R. Kelly.

❧ *My Utmost for His Highest* by Oswald Chambers.

❧ *Readings in St. John's Gospel* by William Temple.

❧ *A Diary of Private Prayer* by John Baillie.

❧ *A Grief Observed* by C. S. Lewis.

❧ *Thoughts in Solitude* and *New Seeds of Contemplation* by Thomas Merton.

❧ *The Wounded Healer, Reaching Out,* and *The Return of the Prodigal Son* by Henri Nouwen.

- Various novels and autobiographical works by Madeleine L'Engle.

- Various novels and autobiographical works by Frederick Buechner.

These are merely some of the writings of the companions of the Spirit whom God has raised up to help us on our way. There are many others. As you begin to read in this field, you will come upon particular authors who seem to write especially for you and your condition. When you find such a one, settle down to make him or her a constant companion, leading you into deeper and richer experiences of your own of the knowledge and love of God.

One final word should be said about spiritual reading. As with the Bible, read *slowly.* This material can be taken into your soul only as you "read, mark, learn, and inwardly digest" it. This means little bites at a time, not entire meals. This is why spiritual reading makes such good bedtime reading. A few pages are enough. But taken regularly over the years these works offer grace and strength for the inner life.

Prayer groups

In union there is strength. When barriers are broken through, power is released. Resources for living are available in relationships between people that a solitary person cannot know. When people pray together, they are given insights they do not receive alone.

A prayer group is nothing more than a group of persons—two or three, ten or twelve—who come together at regular intervals to pray. A mutual giving takes place among people who share their experiences of God and God's spirit resides within them as they move into deeper understanding and love of each other and of God.

Prayer groups are formed for different purposes and center around different concerns. Some may meet to pray for others: the sick, those in special need, communities, political leaders, missions, world peace, racial justice, and other particular causes. Bible study groups, begun and continued in the spirit of prayer, help people relate the meaning of the Bible to their lives and their communities. Other groups may meet for the study of devotional classics or theological books or to share religious experiences. Whatever their nature, prayer groups are at their best when there is a minimum of organization, when no one person dominates, and when each person feels free to bring his or her own contribution of prayer and concern to the group.

If you are one person alone and believe you should belong to a prayer group, begin by praying. Your prayer may be answered in a day or a year, but it will be answered. Sooner or later you will be led to someone or someone will be led to you. Then you have a group to begin. The way *not* to begin a prayer group is to set about organizing one. The only way to begin is to pray. Then God will organize one for you.

The most natural prayer group is the family. God has placed many of us in families and often communicates to us through these family relationships. It is here that we are often first aware of God and first respond to him. It is not simply that "families that pray together stay together," but that in praying they grow toward God. Family prayer can contribute mightily to the spiritual growth of each family member.

Such prayer usually begins with husband and wife responding to God and giving their lives to him. Simple grace at meals is perhaps the easiest way to start, for it provides an opportunity to thank God for his gifts. The next step is often for the couple to thank God for each other. This does not have to be done formally. It is enough that time is shared for personal devotion and that each realizes he or she is being remembered before God by the other and that their life together is being prayed for.

Many couples block out ten minutes during the day. One reads a scripture passage, followed perhaps by prayers or a few paragraphs from a favorite devotional book. Then they pray the Lord's Prayer together and each prays silently for a few moments to conclude. Each couple will discover the pattern most suited for them once they have decided that since God has done so much for them, they will regularly take time to relate their love and life together to him.

This sets the framework within which children can eventually take their places as well. Parents will not only see that their small children have a regular time for prayers and learn such traditional ones as "Now I lay me down to sleep, I pray the Lord my soul to keep," but will include them in family prayer as they grow older. Even quite small children can take their turn in saying table grace. At other times the Bible can be read, thanksgivings offered for blessings received, and prayers said for specific needs.

Only two things are needed by parents for family worship to be significant: a desire to pray and a sense of humor. Family prayer is a time when parental reins of authority should be held loosely and children given the freedom to express what is on their hearts. Often God leads the parents by means of their children. And it will not be in a formal way. The gift of humor is related to the gift of faith, and a family that combines laughter and prayer is close to the kingdom of God.

Retreats
Retreats are times of rest and refreshment away from the place where you carry on your daily activities. A retreat may last for a day or for longer, as people withdraw for quiet, meditation, and prayer, to think through before God the direction of their lives, to regroup their forces, and to return to their lives refreshed and with new perspectives.

A retreat is normally conducted for a group of six or more people who gather either in a monastery, a retreat house established for that purpose, or a conference center adapted for this use. Retreats are arranged either by some sponsoring group or by the center itself. Whatever its nature, a retreat provides an opportunity for physical and psychological rest. For an extended time, you are freed from the daily pressures of living and can begin to slow down your pace.

During a retreat, more attention is given to God than is usually possible in a busy life. It is a time out to take stock. In the traditional retreat, silence is observed. Where no one breaks in on your individual thoughts with trivial comment, you can come to grips with the deep things of God known only in the interior life. With the stilling of other voices, the voice of God can more readily be heard. Usually a retreat conductor provides spoken meditations and conducts worship services that provide a framework for your thoughts and for the guidance of God's spirit. Sometimes individual one-on-one conferences with the retreat leader or another spiritual guide are also part of a retreat. Otherwise, you are alone, yet in the company of like-minded companions, with your thoughts, your reading, your prayers—and your God.

Away from the petty details of an over-busy life, it is possible to be given something of the eternal perspective on your life. Here is help to distinguish between important and unimportant, right and wrong, good and evil. Visions long forgotten can be reclaimed and brought again into focus; broken hopes can be restored, new strength gained, and a fresh confidence in God and his power for your life renewed. Then you return to your daily life, where God has placed you, restored and reinvigorated to meet the demands laid upon you.

If you have never made a retreat, this may be the time to consider whether God is not now placing the opportunity before you to go apart for a time, to be still and know that he is God.

A Rule of Life

The world is very much with us, and the world is strong. It is too strong for us and will engulf us if we are content simply to drift. Our life of prayer will soon disappear if we think it will take care of itself naturally. It will not. The best guarantee that we shall not be engulfed by the world is to adopt what is called a "rule of life."

To adopt a rule of life is simply to conduct our lives according to a chosen standard. It is to acknowledge that the life of prayer and personal religion will grow only as we regularly and devotedly pay attention to it. It is to strengthen our relationship to God through consistent and regular spiritual exercise. To pray simply when we feel like it or "when the spirit moves us" is not enough to build on, for no progress is made when all is left to chance or mood. In adopting a rule of life we commit ourselves to the best way we know of drawing close to God and to stick with it as best we can, come what may.

A rule of life brings stability to the inner life. Living by a rule relieves us of the extremes to which many people resort: one day praying fervently and enthusiastically, and the next suspecting that there is no God and wondering if we did not make fools of ourselves the day before. With a rule, this is settled once and for all. Emotional fluctuations do not intrude because our emotions no longer guide us. When we feel apart from God, we nevertheless quietly continue to pray because we know such moods will pass. We do not trust our moods, but God. When God seems far away, we stay with our rule, undisturbed by passing moods.

As you begin to make a rule of life for yourself, one word of caution must be spoken: *begin with a simple, easy rule.* Beginners in the first flush of enthusiasm often try to take huge strides toward God. They usually tire, soon become discouraged, and often give up the journey altogether. Instead, begin with small, easy steps that you are sure you can handle. Then in time, when you are steady on your feet, enlarge your stride. It is better to begin with a five-minute rule of daily prayer and stick to it than to start with a fifteen-minute commitment that you often neglect.

Inexperienced mountain climbers often exhaust themselves in the first hours as they hurry with long strides up the mountain. Experienced mountaineers, on the other hand, go up the first slopes with short, easy steps—but they keep going. Make your first rule of life a short, simple one. Then after a month or six months, reexamine it and, if you believe it is right, strengthen it. Through the years, reconsidering your rule perhaps once a year, as your spiritual muscles grow stronger through experience, your progress will be steady, secure, and certain.

The one who can best tell you what your rule should be is God. If you pray quietly and consistently to him about a rule, you will come to an inward conviction as to what it should be. A very simple rule to begin with might be this:

1. Pray for five minutes twice a day, using the "five foundation stones" as a guide.

2. Meditate on some passage in the Bible fifteen minutes a week.

3. Do some spiritual reading once a week.

4. Worship God every Sunday and participate in at least one other way in the life of your church.

Many people who begin are doing something like this off and on anyway. The value of the rule is to make it precise and definite, so that beginning at this point, you can then progress in a steady direction. Once your relationship with God is firmly fixed, you can then respond to God and let him lead you into the next steps. They will always be larger steps, but only gradually so.

When a rule of life has been made, it should be observed. This is now the standard by which you determine to conduct your religious life. It is a promise to God that you will move your life in this direction. It serves as a rudder providing purpose and direction to your devotional life. The winds and waves of life that beat upon us are so strong that without some rule the world will ultimately engulf us. A rule of life helps make this impossible.

On Beginning Again

Anyone who has ever made a promise knows how easy it is not to keep it. Prayers promised are forgotten and the rule is broken. What then?

When you have broken your rule and could have kept it (obviously there are times when it is broken unavoidably), simply tell God you are sorry and start again. There is no need to grieve over it or to brood about it, nor, once you have confessed, to feel guilty. This happens to any commitment when we depend upon ourselves to carry it out: we always fall short. We can expect that. So tell God you are sorry and begin again, asking him for his help that you may now keep your rule properly.

The key is in beginning again. That, in fact, is part of what the Christian life is all about, being willing to begin again. We often promise to lead a new life with God's help, then forget God's help and fail. This is the crucial moment. We can give up in despair or we can begin again. The mark of the Christian is to start afresh, patiently and in good cheer and hope. The Christian life is a series of new beginnings.

The only sin God cannot deal with is the sin of giving up. When we throw up our hands (and our faith) in despair and say, "There is no answer to my problem; God has no power to help and save; there is no hope for me," then we have plunged into the sin of despair. To give up utterly is deliberately to cut ourselves off from God. Then God can do nothing—until we turn again to him and cry, "Help me!" or "Forgive me!" or just simply, "Lord, I have returned; here I am." This is to begin again.

At the other end of the scale, God can do nothing when we believe we have all the answers or need nothing more from God. This is the sin of self-righteousness and pride. God can only break through this sin when we turn to him and say, "I am sorry. Forgive me. There is no health in me." Then we can begin again and enter once more into the joy of an open, clean relationship with God, knowing ourselves to be forgiven sinners and confidently beginning a new life with him.

The sum of the matter is that as Christians we acknowledge ourselves frankly for what we are—frail, weak creatures, trying to lead our lives as we believe God wants us to, but often falling down and failing in even the simplest of moral acts. The power that tempts us to failure, to sin, and to life away from God is so strong that we deliberately adopt some rule to keep us on course.

Failure does not surprise or discourage us, for we know to expect it without God's help. So we simply express our sorrow for having failed and begin again. This time perhaps we will be faithful to our rule one day longer and we thank God for the added help he has given us. And we begin the next stage the next day. But whether we succeed for long periods or stumble day by day, our rule of life keeps our direction toward God. When we succeed, we praise God. When we fail, we pick ourselves up and start again.

And always we go our way rejoicing, confident, expectant, hopeful, encouraged. No terrors frighten us, no dangers destroy us, no evil can finally harm us. We are pilgrims and we are on our way. We rejoice in all that God has done for us in the past, confident that as we know him now as our Companion along the way, we shall one day see him face to face. We say with Augustine: "Now therefore, my brothers, let us sing, not for our delight as we rest, but to cheer us in our labor. Sing as wayfarers sing, but keep marching." This is to live as a Christian, beginning each day, again and again and again.

CHAPTER 7

Mature Personal Religion:
Action and Worship

Someone has rightly said that a person's best prayer is what he does when he is not praying. Important as religious activities are, our religion is shown in our day-to-day decisions, in the ordinary experiences of life. Mature personal religion recognizes that our relationship to God is reflected in and influenced by our *living*.

This means that our actions are a *result* of our prayers. If our attention to God does not mean more loving attention to other people, something is seriously wrong with our prayers. The results of our prayers are seen in our lives. It also means that what we do *prepares* us for prayer. We cannot live in sin and expect to live with God. How we spend our time outside of prayer determines whether we are closer to God or farther away from him when we turn to prayer. The person who draws nearest to God is the one who returns with clean hands and a pure heart.

What we do, then, is both a result of and a preparation for prayer. It is also the surest indication of the maturity of our religion. A person of mature faith sees that her personal religion is not simply a compartment of life, but animates all her life.

GUIDES FOR ACTION

God is not especially, or even primarily, interested in our "religious" activities; God is concerned with *all* our activities. We show our response to God by our actions throughout the week as well as on Sundays; in our hours of employment and leisure as well as in our hours of worship; in the way we treat the members of our family as well as the way we usher in church. God is as concerned with how much money we spend on luxuries as with the amount we give to the church; with our sex life as with our prayer life; with the control of our temper and talents as with our piety and devotions. There is no area of life that is not subject to the Lord of all life.

Our behavior toward others is the heart of personal religion. Although religion is more than morality, if our religion does not guide us in our moral decisions, it is inadequate and finally harmful. Three little words can guide our actions and point to the way God would have us behave. They are duty, love, and justice. We shall look briefly at each.

To begin with *duty* is simply to say that our first obligation is to pay the debts we already owe. In most experiences, God calls us simply to go about our business and carry out our duties. Each of us is involved in a whole network of relationships which can be maintained and strengthened only as we discharge our obligations.

Indeed, there are times when a sense of duty is the only thing holding together all the broken pieces of our lives. For most of us, most of the time, it is a sense of duty that gives us direction and purpose. Not only our personal relationships, but the structure of society itself is held together as we carry out our duties to one another, as we keep our pledged word—even though it be to our own hurt. This is the first level of Christian morality.

The relationship between husband and wife in Christian *love* is the most obvious illustration of the next level. The concern of each is always for the other. There is an outgoing care and direction that absorbs differences of opinion and emotional upheavals. Each partner knows that the central thing in the relationship is that he or she is loved by the other. This experience of being loved in turn helps both partners to love all the more in response. Morality in personal relationships always acts for the good of the other person.

Society, however, is largely impersonal. It is simply impossible to enter into personal relationships with many people. A Christian father, for example, may know how to express his love for his wife and children, perhaps even for his next-door neighbor. But how can he express this same love in such complex social issues as war and peace, full employment and wages, race relations, public housing, stewardship of the environment, and immigration policy? Yet he is called upon to act as a Christian citizen on just such issues as these.

So the final guide is *justice*. In all the impersonal relationships of society, we as Christians will support forces that seem to promise a more just and humane social order. They may be "Christian" forces or they may not. We will seek to strengthen parties, causes, and groups which, in our best judgment, will make it easier for people to love their neighbors as themselves. We will not be discouraged because the perfect society of love seems far off, but will work for approximate goals so as to contribute to a more just social order. Someone has said that justice is love working at long range; impersonal social forces working for justice are the expression of persons motivated by love.

The guides for action, then, in both our personal and our impersonal relationships, arise out of the principles of duty, love, and justice. These provide the framework within which we carry out our personal religion and reveal its strength.

Worship as the Central Act

Personal religion also means *worship*. Worship is our central act toward God. It may include praise and thanksgiving, confession, petition and intercession, or all these elements together. Mature personal religion involves not only personal prayer and social action, but also *corporate* worship. Corporate worship is the action not of a person but of a *people*, bound together in a special relationship to each other and to God.

We considered in chapters 1 and 2 how the Spirit of God touches us through nature, our search for truth, beauty, and goodness, our unmet needs. As we respond to this Spirit, the meaning of our life under God grows clearer to us. But there is more than that. The Spirit finally leads us to other people, to the *community* of those who know who they are because they know who God is. Members of this community know they are God's children because they first know God as Father, and in them is seen the truth about *all* people—*all* are children of the one Father. Jesus Christ is at the center of this community; it is where he is confessed, adored, and worshiped. This community is the church.

This is not the place to describe how all this came to be. It is enough to point out that God has always dealt with people in terms of their relationships with one another. He chose the Jewish *people,* made a covenant with them, and called the whole people to respond faithfully to him. The Old Testament is the story of how God chose them, led them, delivered them, loved them, pleaded with them, forgave them, and remained always faithful to them. God chose the Jews so that through them he might make himself known to all people.

When the Jews repeatedly fell short in this mission, God sent his Son to establish a new covenant or relationship, settling once and for all the issue between a holy God and guilty humanity. Jesus Christ taught, healed, preached. Then, on the cross, on behalf of all of us, he offered a full, perfect, and sufficient sacrifice, oblation, and satisfaction for the sins of the whole world. This shows how much God loved the world—so much that only the sacrifice or offering of his Son could express it.

This, then, is the heart of the mystery of God: *love in action is sacrifice.* The cross on which the body of Christ is broken points to what heals the broken relationship between humanity and God. The cross links us below to God above. It derives its power from the offering of the perfect Man and perfect God. So the whole mysterious enterprise is built on sacrificing love. Sacrifice is as high and deep as eternity, and wholly reveals what God is like.

When Jesus left our sight and returned to his Father to intercede continually for us, he gave his Spirit to the world. This is the Spirit who has touched us in so many ways down through the ages. As people have responded, they have been drawn into the family of God, the church.

This is not to say that Christians are better than other people. Sadly, sometimes we are worse. It is to say that as Christians, we know who we are and that God has chosen us to live as members of his family for a purpose: that *everyone* may discover who they are, too. The church is bound together through time and space by God's Spirit, where his Son Jesus Christ is known and confessed, and whose central act is the worship of God in the name of his Son.

As the heart of God's action toward us is the sacrifice of the cross, so the heart of our response to God is also sacrifice—the sacrifice of worship. Love is at the center of it. Love in action always issues in sacrifice. Worship is an offering of sacrifice to God—we offer ourselves and one another in the great prayer of the church for all people. Our prayer is joined to the prayer of Christ who continually intercedes for us. By virtue of who he is, we dare make our offerings to God and our intercessions for one another and for the world.

Most of all, however, Christians present *the offering of Christ himself.* Since worship is an action toward God, inspired by his Spirit, its meaning is disclosed *sacramentally.* A sacrament is an outward and visible sign of an inward and spiritual grace. We see this most clearly in the central act of Christian worship—the breaking of bread and the drinking of wine. This is ordinary bread and wine, but it *signifies* to us—is the *sign* of—the body and blood of Christ, offered first for us, then by us. We pray that as we recall and remember Jesus, his Spirit will make us partakers of his body and blood. So through outward signs, we receive Christ spiritually to the refreshing and strengthening of our souls.

The Christian family in this action recalls—calls back—that living sacrifice or offering which was made once and for all on Calvary. This was the great offering of Christ himself for the world. It is continually being made by him. Our offering of ourselves, our alms and oblations, bread and wine, is joined to his and *in his name* is accepted by God.

This offering of Christ's is the heart of the church's worship. As members of the church, we are incorporated into his eternal offering and by virtue of it we make our own offering in our particular time and place. The eternal and invisible and spiritual are given outward and visible signs in this act of corporate worship. By participating in it, by receiving Christ's body and blood, we are strengthened to become more and more what we already are and what was declared by the sacramental action of baptism: members of Christ, children of God, and inheritors of the kingdom of heaven.

Mature Christian living, then, is to love God and one another. It is a life of action and of worship. Since the action of love always issues in sacrifice and the heart of worship is sacrificial action, all of life for the Christian is of a piece. Whether in our daily activities or in our religious devotion, our life is an offering of love. Responding to the great love of God given in Christ, in whom is our hope for eternity, we offer to God and each other all that we are and all that we do. Whether we live or die, we are the Lord's. And whatever we do, we do it as for him.

A Christian does nothing except for the glory of God. If this is what we seek, then all our action and worship will glorify God. This is the meaning of mature personal religion: "to glorify God, and to enjoy him forever." So let us finally turn to that joy which is our intended end.

CHAPTER 8

On Suffering and Joy

Man was made for joy and woe;
And, when this we rightly know,
Safely through the world we go.

. . . .

Joy and woe are woven fine,
A clothing for the soul divine.

—WILLIAM BLAKE, "AUGURIES OF INNOCENCE"

At the heart of the Christian life lies a great mystery: suffering and joy are inextricably bound together. The absence of suffering does not bring joy; indeed, the only abiding joy arises out of what we do with our suffering. The path to joy is discovered as sufferings are accepted for the love of God. The greatest joy of all, for the Christian, is in knowing that as he gladly embraces his sufferings for the love of God, he offers his most potent prayer to release the power of God in the world.

This does not mean, as we have already seen, that we are to accept evil or suffering complacently and make no effort to remove their causes. On the contrary, as Christians, we are to fight against them unceasingly. Nor is this to say that God sends suffering to particular persons as punishment for their sins. But since sin and suffering, disease and death are here, it does mean that God permits them and that we must reckon with them. They may be the only means whereby we come to know God and experience his joy. It is like a surgeon who allows us to suffer the pain of an operation in order that we may get well.

To see this more clearly, we must consider two questions: *How are we meant to respond to all life that is given us? And how are we to respond in particular to the sufferings that are given, when everything has been done, humanly speaking, to remove them?*

The answer to the first question provides a framework for the second. It is quite simple: We are to recognize that all life is a gift—life is sheer grace; all comes from God. As we accept all life from him and in our prayers and actions offer it back to him, we begin to share in God's divine purpose for ourselves and for the world.

Ignatius of Loyola in the sixteenth century expressed it this way: "Take, Lord, and receive my liberty, my memory, my understanding, my will—all that I have and possess. You, Lord, have given all to me. I now give it back to you, O Lord. All of it is yours. Dispose of it according to your will. Give me love of yourself along with your grace, for that is enough for me."

If this prayer expresses our attitude toward life, God, and all that life brings, we have an undercurrent of zest, excitement, and purpose that cannot be destroyed, whatever comes. We will be in the midst of life and glad to be there, even when the waters are turbulent. We will understand that all of life comes from God, that God is present where we are, and that we are to respond to him as best we can, offer everything back to him, and carry on for him. In this way we discover joy as the enduring experience of all life. God gives joy as we respond in this way to what life brings and lifts our spirits in all things and circumstances.

Most of us can approach this attitude when life is going smoothly and presents no great difficulties. It is another matter, however, when things go wrong, when obstacles block our way, and when we suffer unexpected and undeserved hardships. Yet it is here, especially here, that the path to joy is discovered. So we turn to the second question: *How are we to respond to sufferings when we have done everything to remove them?*

The secret is to accept our sufferings joyfully for the love of God. This is not at all like gritting our teeth to endure them in a spirit of resignation. To accept sufferings willingly and gladly is to help Christ release God's power in the world to combat evil and sin and suffering. This is to share in a measure the same joy that was set before Christ, for which he endured the cross.

The most powerful prayer is to take our sufferings for the love of God, offer them to him, and then carry them as crosses to be borne joyfully for Christ's sake. An abiding joy and enduring peace are held out for us when we suffer in this way and come to see purpose and meaning in our sufferings.

When pain and agony, either physical or mental or
spiritual, come upon us and we have tried every human
means to alleviate them and still they remain, we pray
like this: "O God, I do not understand why this is
happening to me. I only know that it is here and I cannot
avoid it. You permit it to happen to me for a purpose I
cannot now discern. Therefore, in your sight and as
honestly as I can, I take it into myself for the sake of
Christ who suffered for me. And now with him I offer it
and myself back to you, knowing that you will do with
it and with me whatever is right and good. In your good
time and in your own way, you will make clear that your
way is the best way, and I shall then know the reason
why. In the meantime, you will not give me anything to
endure without the strength also to bear it. I pray that in
my dealings now with others, I may show something of
the fruit of your Spirit, that through me they may be led
to you. Give me, then, your grace for today, that in some
measure I may be gentle, peaceful, joyful, long-suffering,
good, meek, temperate, full of faith and love. So I thank
you for the trust you now show toward me. I promise to
hang on and trust in you alone, come what may; through
Jesus Christ my Lord. Amen."

It is not merely that this kind of prayer gives us grace
and strength to accept our own sufferings. Every act of
joyful acceptance of suffering for the love of God releases
a power into the world that helps all people carry their
crosses. Every such act sets free one more channel for
the power of God in people's lives, releasing strength for
everyone carrying on their own battle against temptation, sin, or suffering. In this way we help marshal the
resources of God in his continuing struggle against all
that is evil and wrong in the world. Our individual

response to him, embracing our suffering and love of him, makes his Spirit more available for all people in their particular struggles.

Consider, for example, a father who is suddenly struck with a disease that his doctors say will be fatal within five years. He has a wife and four children. As news of his illness spreads, former friends from every chapter of his life come to visit him. After a year in bed during which he has battled courageously and accepted his illness graciously, he can say: "I am not yet sure why this should have happened to me, but already I can say that more good has come out of it than evil. Because of this, all my relationships, even the snarled and broken ones, have been straightened out and healed. All are now full of grace. Whatever may happen now, I thank God for his goodness to me in letting this come to me." The father found joy through suffering, and this enabled him to give power and grace for their own struggles to all whose lives he touched.

Mental and spiritual suffering is sometimes harder to bear than physical pain, but the same joy found through suffering is discovered there as well. Here is the story of a woman who through the most intense personal suffering was led to the joy of the Christian life and in the process so touched the lives of others that they too were encouraged on their way. She felt shattered when her husband announced one day that he planned to divorce her and leave her with two young children. She suddenly discovered that all that she had valued and depended upon was now not enough. Although she had no religious faith to begin with, she was helped by Christian friends to see that condemning her husband would lead nowhere and that her first responsibility was to look within herself to see what she might learn from this experience and outside herself to God for help. After months of inner struggle, she gave herself to God fully and wholly. Soon afterward she found employment, and from her first small paycheck gave ten percent as a "thank offering to God for being so good to me."

Now years later, she has matured into a woman of profound Christian faith, with an unshakeable conviction that "all things work together for good for those who love God" (Romans 8:28), and is a living witness that with Christ one can do all things. Others now turn to her for counsel, guidance, and strength when suffering comes to them. "It is the miracle of God's grace," she writes, "that not until I almost died with pain at what had happened was I able at first barely to get up and stumble on, but then in time to rejoice that this suffering had come to me. This was the gate I had to go through to discover the abiding peace and joy that God holds out for those who trust in him. So now, while I miss my husband, of course, I still can thank God for his great and undeserved goodness to me." She had discovered that suffering taken and offered back to God is the way to joyful and fruitful living.

The reason suffering joyfully for the love of God is so powerful is that this is the way of the cross. It is the way Christ did his work. Not only in his living and teaching and healing, but finally in his dying on the cross he redeemed the world. The world is a different place because Christ accepted joyfully his sufferings for the love of God.

We are part of this great work of redemption. As we accept our sufferings joyfully for the love of God, the world again becomes a different place. This is to have some part—a small part, but our part—in Christ's great act of redemption. It is to make available for everyone our share in his Spirit. There is therefore no such thing as "useless" suffering. Suffering for God, in the spirit of Christ, is the most "useful" thing a person can do. Long-term sufferers are potentially the most useful citizens in God's kingdom. Every ounce of suffering accepted in this way is transformed by God into power and released to his glory and for the good of his people.

Such is the path to joy. There is no greater joy than to know that you are a partaker with Christ in the work God intends for him and for all members of his body. This is to serve on earth him from whom you came, to whom you belong, and with whom you shall live forever. It is for this that you were born.

This joy is not confined to our life on earth. It is also part of life in heaven, shared by all who live with God and offer him their sacrifice of praise and thanksgiving. In joyfully adoring God, the whole company of heaven helps release the power of God's Spirit for us in our earthly pilgrimage.

There is no sharp division, therefore, between our life as Christians now and our life with God and his people after death, for nothing, not even death, can separate us from God's love in Christ for us. The heart of that life is action for the love of God, and worship in praise of him. This means suffering joyfully for his sake on earth, and it brings with it a foretaste of that perfect joy that shall be ours in heaven. This joy is the love of God in our hearts now and forever.

Whether on earth or in heaven, then, we join our song to the song of angels and archangels and the whole company of heaven: "Holy, holy, holy Lord, God of power and might, heaven and earth are full of your glory. Hosanna in the highest."

✝

Discussion
Questions

*Note: The following questions may be useful to individuals
reading this book in search of a deeper life of prayer, or they
may form the basis for discussions by study groups. Study
groups may wish to combine two or more chapters in a single
session. These questions were prepared by the late Mrs.
Marcus J. Priester of Lansdowne, Pennsylvania, and the Rev.
Dr. Richard H. Schmidt of Cincinnati, Ohio.*

✝

Chapter 1
Prayer Is Response to God

   ✢   What experiences can you identify as times
when God sought to speak to you or influence you?
How did you respond?

   ✢   What visual images of God are in your mind?
To what human figure do you most easily compare

God? What does this say about your understanding of God's character and disposition toward you?

 As you understand the person of God, is God someone to whom you really *want* to be in relationship?

 Make the suggested list of good things in your life for which God is responsible.

 Make the suggested list of bad things in your life which God permits, and ask yourself why God permits them.

✝

Chapter 2
Be Yourself and Begin Where You Are

 About what in your life is it hardest for you to be honest with God?

 What would you like to say to God but hesitate to say? Why do you hesitate?

 Is the desire for peace of mind, power for living, or forgiveness the thing that most moves you toward God? Or is it something else?

 If "selfish" prayer is permissible, can prayer become too selfish?

 Complete these sentences: O God, help me to.... Forgive me for.... Thank you for....

✝

Chapter 3
Clearing the Ground

 Do you agree that the time and place of prayer are relatively unimportant? What time and place work for you?

 How do you use printed prayers from devotional literature? Can they be a detriment in prayer?

 Choose a short psalm and rewrite it in your own words.

✝

Chapter 4
The Foundation Stones of Prayer

 Think of the prayers you pray. Which of the five kinds of prayer discussed in this chapter are they? Is there one kind of prayer that you neglect?

 Make a list of things you are thankful for. Be specific.

 How is it possible to be thankful amid suffering and tragedy?

 How are "sins of the flesh" and "sins of the spirit" related? Give an example.

 How would you respond to someone who declared that "God did not answer my prayer"?

"Not my will but yours be done," Jesus prayed just before his crucifixion. What does this prayer tell us about Jesus? If we pray this prayer, how will it affect our other prayers?

✝

Chapter 5
The House That Prayer Builds

 What are some of the obstacles to developing a way of meditating that does not become dry intellectualism or mere ritual? How do you remove these obstacles?

 Try visualizing a biblical scene like the one in which Peter meets Jesus that was discussed in this chapter. Take time to do it; do not hurry through it. Is this helpful to you?

 Both emotional dryness and emotional excess can detract from a healthy prayer life. When have you experienced one or both? How do you guard against them?

 Do you really want to be intimate with God, or does that idea frighten you?

Chapter 6
Progress in Prayer

 What is your biggest stumbling block in the way of practicing the presence of God?

 List three ways you can become more attentive to God during the busy times of your day. Choose one of them and do it for a week.

 Find a short meditation, scripture passage, or prayer and read it slowly, several times, letting the words filter quietly through your soul. If you do not know of such a passage, try a few verses from Psalm 46, Isaiah 55, Romans 12, or 1 Corinthians 13.

 Do you pray with your spouse or significant other? If not, what causes you to hold back?

 Make a rule of life and keep it intentionally for a week. Remember: begin with a simple, easy rule.

Chapter 7
Mature Personal Religion: Action and Worship

 If "God is not especially, or even primarily, interested in our 'religious' activities," why do we engage in religious activities?

 Identify something you do as an expression of (1) your sense of duty, (2) your Christian love, and (3) your understanding of justice.

❧ How are duty, love, and justice related to one another in practice?

❧ What is there about Christian worship that makes it an act of sacrifice?

❧ What distinguishes a Christian from someone who is not a Christian but seeks to live an upright life?

✝

Chapter 8
On Suffering and Joy

❧ What experiences in your life point to the mystery that "suffering and joy are inextricably bound together"?

❧ Is there suffering that should not be "gladly" embraced?

❧ If "there is no such thing as 'useless' suffering," what is the use of suffering?

❧ Madeleine L'Engle said: "Virtue is not the sign of a Christian. Joy is." What is the source of this joy?